Kailash Journal

Pilgrimage in the Sacred Himalayas of Tibet

Books by Sri Swami Satchidananda

Beyond Words
Enlightening Tales
The Golden Present
Healing From Disaster
The Healthy Vegetarian
Heaven on Earth

Integral Yoga Hatha
Kailash Journal
The Living Gita
To Know Your Self
Satchidananda Sutras
Yoga Sutras of Patanjali

Books/Films about Sri Swami Satchidananda

The Master's Touch
Sri Swami Satchidananda: Apostle of Peace
Sri Swami Satchidananda: Portrait of a Modern Sage
Boundless Giving: The Life and Service of Sri Swami Satchidananda
Living Yoga: The life and teachings of Swami Satchidananda
Many Paths, One Truth: The Interfaith Message of Swami Satchidananda
The Essence of Yoga: The Path of Integral Yoga with Swami Satchidananda

For complete listing of books, CDs and DVDs: www.iydbooks.com

Library of Congress Cataloging in Publication Data

Satchidananda, Swami.
Kailash journal.
"Originally published in the Tamil language."

1. Hindu pilgrims and pilgrimages – China – Kailash Mountain.
2. Hindu pilgrims and pilgrimages – Himalaya Mountains Region.
3. Himalaya Mountains Region – Description and travel.
4. Satchidananda, Swami.

I. Title.

BL1239.38.C62K35713   1984   294.5'446   84-25296
ISBN 978-0-932040-25-1

Printed in the United States of America.

Integral Yoga® Publications
Satchidananda Ashram–Yogaville
108 Yogaville Way, Buckingham, Virginia, USA 23921
www.YogaAndPeace.org

Kailash Journal

Pilgrimage in the Sacred
Himalayas of Tibet

By
Sri Swami Satchidananda

With photographs
by the author

Originally published in the Tamil language
English translation by Sri P. Shanmugam
With a new foreword by Graham Schweig, Ph.D.
and a new introduction by Rev. Kumari de Sachy, Ed.D.

Front cover photo by Matthew Reichel

Integral Yoga® Publications

I worship that fullness, which pervades as awareness, which is omnipresent as beauty and which eternally blesses with blissful joy.

Holy Mount Kailash

Master and disciple: His Holiness Sri Swami Sivananda Maharaj of the Himalayas and the author.

Divine Life Society

Founder & President
Sri Swami Sivananda

Sivananda Nagar, Rishikesh
Himalayas, India

Blessings

OM Namo Narayanaya!

My blessings to you all. My disciple Swami Satchidananda is well-known for the tremendous service he renders to the cause of the Lord. His work is commendable. He is a Karma Yogi who puts the saying "My purpose is to serve" into continual practice.

Kailash Journal is one of the publications written by him. He has expressed the joyful experience of pilgrimage and the vision of the Lord in simple, lucid language, understandable by all. In the vast field of literature, this book stands out as exemplary.

The photographs and day-by-day descriptions give the reader the divine feeling of participation in the journey. Thus, while reading, we too become travelers and can experience the benefits of this holy pilgrimage. May each one be filled with the blessings of the Lord of Kailash.

Om Shanti! Shanti! Shanti!
May peace be unto all!

Your own self,
SWAMI SIVANANDA

Contents

Chapter 1:   1
Pilgrimage; The Obstacle Race; Departure to Kailash;
The Truths Revealed There.

Chapter 2:   5
The Decision to Go; It Will Not Be Possible to Dine as Usual;
More Hints; To Ensure Success; Farewell; An Auspicious Delay; The Pilgrims Gather.

Chapter 3:   13
Bus Ride from Kathkodam; The View from the Bus;
The Himalayan Range; Physical Wealth; Spiritual Wealth.

Chapter 4:   17
Raniket: Even the Pavement is Beautiful; Almora: Popular and Peaceful;
The Treasures of Almora; The Streets of Heaven; Firmness is Needed; Many Paths
to One Goal; We Get a Guide and a Friend; The Mountains Set an Example.

Chapter 5:   23
Bhageswaram; Markandayar Rock; The Joy of Bhageswaram; A Buffalo Will
Not Substitute for the Ego; *Ramayana*; The Start of the Pilgrimage on Foot;
It is Time We Started; A Very Narrow River.

Chapter 6:   29
Has This a Name?; Who Am I?; Bridge of Life; Potholes in Our Beds;
Gasping for Breath; Pethuli Cave: A Rare Opportunity; We Meet a Fox;
A Mother of the Hill Tribe.

Chapter 7:   37
Rethi; Honey from the Hills; Action and Reaction; No Watcher and No
Theft; Nehar and Cold; Nanda Devi Poses.

Chapters: 8   43
Milam: An Unscheduled Stop; The School at Milam; Milam Glacier;
Lake Sandilya: A Blissful Night; Lake Surya Kundam; Some Useful Plants.

Chapter 9:   51
The Hospitality of the Hill Tribes; A Tale from the Past;
Guru Poornima: A Grand Celebration; "Sinnu Munnu";
A Storm Amidst the Calm; May Such Kindness Live Forever.

Chapter 10:   57
More Demands on Behalf of the Mules;
Undathura Pass: Ice and Cold at 18,500 Feet; Life in the Tent.

List of Photographs

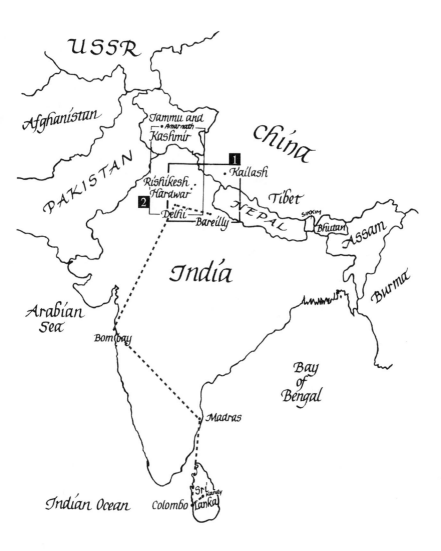

Dotted line: Pilgrimage Route

Map of India from the 1950s. Drawn by Uma Knight.

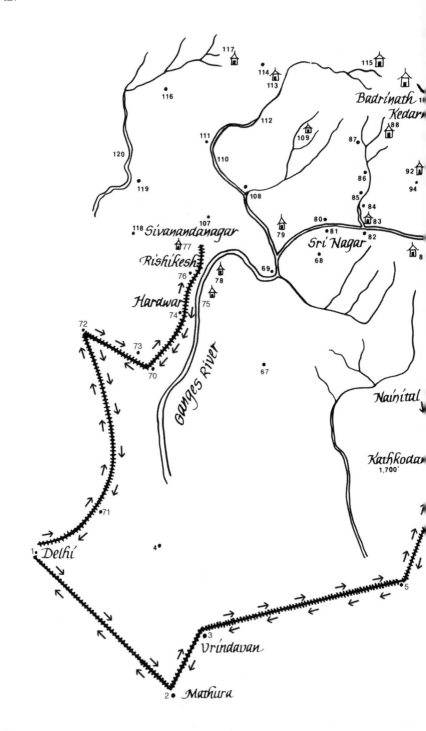

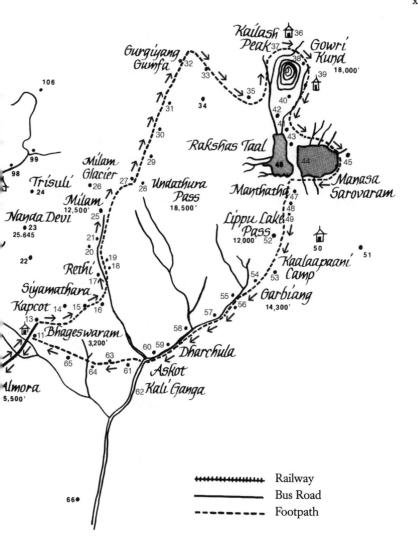

Kailash Peak 🛕36
37
38
Gowri Kund 18,000'
39
🛕

Gurgiyang Gumfa •32
33
35

106
31
•34
30
40
42
41
43

Milam Glacier
29
Rakshas Taal
45
44
48

99
98
27• 28
Undathura Pass 18,500'
Manthatha 47
Manasa Sarovaram

Trisuli •24
•26
48
49
Lippu Lake Pass 12,000' 52
Milam 12,500'
25•

Nanda Devi •23 25.645
🛕
50
51

21•
20
Kaalaapaani Camp
54 53

22 •
19
•18
55 •
Garbiang 14,300'
56

Rethi
17
57

Siyamathara
16
58

Kapcot 14 • 15 • 16
•11
Bhageswaram 3,200'
13•
🛕
60 59
Dharchula
65
63
64 61
Askot
62 *Kali Ganga*

Almora 5,500'

66•

┼┼┼┼┼┼┼┼┼┼┼ Railway
─────── Bus Road
─ ─ ─ ─ ─ ─ Footpath

Kailash Pilgrimage: Box 1 from Map of India on page xiii

Pilgrimage Key

Stops along pilgrimage to Mount Kailash and Amarnath Cave, as well as some of the other notable places in the region.

1. Delhi
2. Mathura
3. Vrindavan
4. Happur
5. Bareilly
6. Lalgufa
7. Kathkodam
8. Nainital (return trip)
9. Raniket
10. Almora
11. **Bhageswaram**
12. **Bhaijnath**
13. Kapcot
14. Siyamathara
15. Quintee
16. Girham
17. Rethi
18. Rupshibagar
19. Bagutyar
20. Nehar
21. Martholi
22. Pindari Glacier
23. Nanda Devi
24. Trisuli
25. Milam
26. Milam Glaciers
27. Mala Shilong
28. Undathura Pass
29. Dobithunga
30. Palche Pass
31. Kemlung
32. **Gurgiyang Gumfa**
33. **Thirthapuri**
34. Jnanimamundi
35. **Landi Gumfa**
36. **Dorafuk Gumfa**
37. **Kailash Peak**
38. **Gowri Kund**
39. **Jentalfuk Gumfa**
40. Sindhu River
41. Dharchan
42. **Gnyandang Gumfa**
43. **Ju Gumfa**
44. **Manasa Sarovaram**
45. **Tokkar Gumfa**
46. **Rakshas Taal**
47. Manthatha
48. Kurla Pass
49. Takla Kot
50. **Kocharnath**
51. Muktinath Pass
52. Lippu Lake Pass
53. Kaalaapaani Camp
54. Garbiang
55. Bukti
56. Maalpa
57. Jipthi
58. Yela
59. Dharchula
60. Palawa Kot
61. Askot
62. Kali Ganga

63. Didihuc
64. Dhal
65. Bijapur
66. Tanakpur
67. Kodwara
68. Bowri
69. **Ganga (Ganges) River**
70. Laksar
71. Mirat
72. Saharanpur
73. Rurki
74. **Hardwar**
75. Chandi Devi Temple
76. **Rishikesh**
77. **Sivanandanagar**
78. **Swargashram**
79. **Devaprayag**
80. Kirtinagar
81. Sri Nagar
82. Gulabraai
83. **Rudraprayag**
84. Agasthyamuni
85. Mandagini River
86. Guptakasi
87. **Triyuganarayan**
88. **Kedarnath**
89. **Karnaprayag**
90. Kanain
91. Chamoli

92. **Gopeshwara**
93. **Rudranath**
94. **Tunganath**
95. **Jyotir Math**
96. **Vishnuprayag**
97. **Bhavishya Badri**
98. Alakanda River
99. Malari
100. **Pandukeshwar**
101. Vishnu Ganga
102. Lokpal Lake
103. **Badrinath**
104. Mana Village
105. Mana Pass
106. Nithi Pass
107. Narendranagar
108. Tehri
109. **Buddha Kedar**
110. **Bagirati River**
111. Darasu
112. **Uttara Kashi**
113. Mala
114. Todital
115. **Gangothri**
116. Chimini
117. **Yamunothri**
118. Dehra Dun
119. Massoori
120. **Yamuna River**

Boldface: Holy places–shrines, holy *madams* and holy waters (rivers)
Numbers refer to places identified on map of Kailash pilgrimage on
the following pages.

Itinerary

Kailash Trip

May	15	1958	Dep: Kandy	Arr:	Colombo	Train
	16		Colombo		Madras	Plane
	19		Madras		Bombay (20th)	Train
	22		Bombay		Delhi (23rd)	Train
	24		Delhi		Rishikesh	Train
June	1		Rishikesh		Delhi	Train
June	2		Delhi, Mathura, Vrindavan, Lalgufa, Bareilly			Train
	3	1,700'	Kathkodam			Bus
		6,000'	Raniket			Bus
	4	5,500'	Almora			Bus
	5	6,060'	Kowsani			Bus
		3,200'	Bhageswaram			Bus
	8	3,750'	Kapcot; after 3½ miles road forks to Pindari and Milam Glaciers			

Start Journey on Foot (Depart: June 8th)

9	7,000'	Siyamathara (11½ miles from Kapcot)
11	4,000'	Quintee (8 miles)
12	9,000'	Girham (7 miles)
13		Pethuli
14	5,000'	Rethi (9 miles)
16		Rupshibagar or Sundara Medu (11 miles)
		Bagutyar
17	8,000'	Nehar
18	12,222'	Martholi
		Trisuli and Nanda Devi Peaks
19	12,500'	Milam
22	13,000'	Milam Glacier
23		Surya Kund, Sandilya Kund
24	12,500'	Milam
July 1	12,500'	Milam on Guru Poornima
2		Mala Shilong
3	18,500'	Undathura Pass
4		Gangapaani
6		Dobithunga, Sumnath, Kinguru Pass, Lipthal

8		Palche Pass, Jangu (inside Tibet now)
9		Salthu River bank, Sivasailim
11		First Kailash Darshan Day
		Sutlej River bank
12		Kemlung Plateau, Gurgiyang Gumfa
14		Thirthapuri
15		Saashak Plateau, Karlap River bank
16		Landi Gumfa
18		Dorafuk Gumfa: 19,000-foot climb
		(dedication page photo taken from here)
	18,000'	Gowri Kund, Jentalfuk Gumfa
19	16,000'	Dharchan
20		Dharchan: Gnyandang Gumfa
21		A river bank
22		Manasa Sarovaram
24		Dachchu
25		Tokkar Gumfa
26		Karnali River
27		A river bank
28		Takla Kot, Maakram, Pala
29	12,000'	Lippu Pass, Kaalaapaani
30	14,300'	Garbiang (Indian border village)
31		Bukti
August 1	8,000'	Maalpa, Jipthi
2		Sardaali Sardhaan
3	7,000'	Pangu, Yela
4		Dharchula
5		Palawa Kot
6		Kali Ganga, Askot
7		Narayan Nagar, Didihut, Dhal
8		Sakodi, Kumodi, Bijapur
8		Bhageswaram

End of Journey on Foot (Arrival August 8th)

10		Kathkodam	Bus
11		Nainital, Mathura, Delhi	

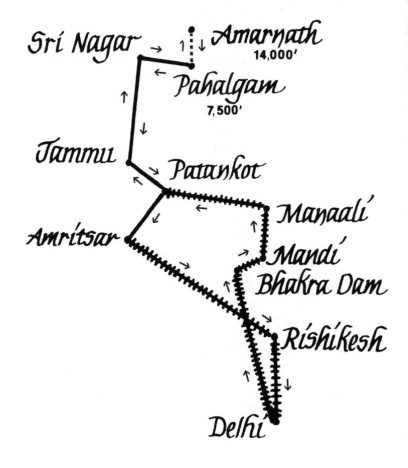

Amarnath Pilgrimage: Box 2 from Map of India on page xiii

Amarnath Pilgrimage

August	16	1958	Leave Delhi, Kurukshetra, Bhakra	
			Nangal Dam, Manaali, Patankot	Train
			Jammu, Sri Nagar	Bus
	25	7,500'	Pahalgam	Foot
	26	9,500'	Chandanwari	
	27		Vaavjaan	
	28	14,700'	Mahagunas Pass	
		13,000'	Pancharharani	
	29	14,000'	Amarnath Cave	
			Pancharharani, Vaavjaan	
	30		Pahalgam	
Aug. 31-Sep.	5		Jammu, Patankot, Amritsar	Bus/Train
September	8		Rishikesh: Sivananda Jayanthi	Train
	10		Delhi	Train
			Bombay, Madras, Coimbatore,	
			Thiruchirappali	
	23		Jaffna, Colombo	Train/Plane
	29		Kandy	Train

Preface

All of us who have come into this world are ultimately believers. Even those who do not believe in God are still believers; their belief is that God does not exist. But whatever our beliefs, we are all aware that we have not come here by our own will. There is something beyond the grasp of our faculties that has brought us into existence.

Since the beginning of time, there have been those who sought to know this mysterious source of life. It has been called Father, Mother, Spirit, Truth, Love, Peace, Consciousness, Suchness and Nothingness. Descriptions such as these provide a starting point from which to begin the search. However, since all seekers are actually looking for the same thing, they very often refer to the object of their quest by a more universal name. That name is "God," and the name itself is treated with great respect to show that the being it represents is much greater in scope, knowledge and power than we are. As most of us have already experienced, He (in reality neither He, She nor It) also has a much stronger will. Truly the Lord of all, this Mysterious One reigns supreme.

Although He can be found anywhere, His seekers choose to look for Him in certain places, because His presence is more readily experienced there. Mount Kailash in the Himalayan range is one such place. Here, throughout the ages, many saints and sages have sought–and seen–Him.

This humble self was graced to experience that great joy. The Lord drew me there, gave me the experience and saw to it that I returned to share it.

Surely all those who seek Him shall find Him. My sincere wish and prayer is that this book might kindle the desire to seek Him, and also serve as a guide in realizing that desire. May He see fit to fulfill this humble prayer.

Satchidananda Ashram
Yogaville, Virginia, 1984

Yours in the Lord,
SWAMI SATCHIDANANDA

Foreword

When we adore something, when we worship it and love it, we want to turn it all the way around, we want to see it from all angles. When we gaze at a beautiful flower, we admire its whorl and rotate the blossom to admire all the alluring petals surrounding its centerpiece. It is the natural movement of the human eye around a work of art, whether a painting or a sculpture–our eyes want to roam around the focal point. When we look at a gorgeous gem, we turn it to see how all its facets catch the light revealing its purity and brilliance. Indeed, in the *Yoga Sutras*, Patanjali describes our inborn, pure consciousness as something that shines forth like that of a jewel (1.41) and the nature of consciousness as something that turns, which he immediately identifies with the phrase, *chitta-vritti* (1.2).

According to the spiritual traditions of India, when we reach a pilgrimage destination where we encounter an image, a temple or a sacred geography, the divine also loves to see us whirled around it. We encircle it by walking all around its periphery completely, a practice known as *parikrama*, which is translated as "circumambulation." When we encounter the outer world in this way, that world is transformed into an inner world. When we have found that particular place in which the sacred has become manifest, when it has burst forth into the outer world in some physical way that can reach our senses, in a way that can move deeply into the very depths of our spiritual hearts, we have communed with the divine; we have honored what is holy; and we have united with what is sacred. And this is precisely what Swami Satchidananda does. He encircles Mount Kailash (see Chapter 14, the section entitled: "Circling His Abode," and Chapter 15, the section entitled: "*Pradakshina*."), while he honors its highest point, its glorious peak (see Chapter 16, the section entitled: "The Peak of Silver").

In this book, we are invited to join a Yoga master in the daily events and practical details involved in a *yatra*, or pilgrimage–a rigorous and austere journey to Mount Kailash, the mountain that manifests the divine presence of Siva. In his own words and photographs, Swami Satchidananda recorded his journey to this great pilgrimage site. He undertook his pilgrimage in the earlier part of the 20th century, when, at age 44, he was already an accomplished yogi. While many books have been compiled from transcripts of Swami Satchidananda's talks, *Kailash Journal* is the only one that he actually wrote during his lifetime. And it is a diary that so clearly reveals the dedicated mood and attractive personality of this very special soul, as he brings us with him by means of his generous descriptions and photographic depictions of this journey. His simple but poignant and sober language sweetly expresses the spiritual sentiments and reflections that he had along the way.

Sri Swami Satchidananda (Sri Swamiji) takes the reader on a journey into his own profound meditation on what he embraces so deeply within his heart, the ultimate destination of all meditation. As Patanjali so eloquently puts it, "From deep within the heart, pure consciousness is fully realized" (*hridaye chitta-samvit,* 3.35). Sri Swamiji poetically describes this deepest level of meditation as an "incomparable pleasure," as expressed in the following eloquent words:

. . . . that supreme joy of being alive and awake in a garden filled with divine blessings, where one can sit in the shade of His holy feet and drink from the eternal spring of divine love (106).

This journal conveys the profound experiences of a pilgrim who goes to the very depths of his own spiritual-religious tradition, who seeks the very heart of what he practices as a yogi. Like all really worthwhile journeys, this one has its dangers, its trials and its challenges. The effort and strength required is neither for the fainthearted, nor for the weak-minded. Sri Swamiji clearly draws his strength and undaunted determination, not just from the rigorous physical practices of the Yoga that he undertook, but also from the strength and fortitude of a self that is saturated with the presence of the divine, a core that he has sought through his own profound meditation. Moreover, his journey demonstrates that, as pilgrims on the path of Yoga, we do not merely immerse ourselves in Yoga; rather, it is the power of Yoga itself that absorbs us. Yoga is a force independent of our own efforts. Sri Swamiji often expresses this phenomenon when he writes about the "grace" of the divine. May we all draw inspiration from his spiritual strength and his devotion to this grace, so that we, too, may become even more empowered through the *sadhana* (spiritual practice) of Yoga!

Swami Satchidananda demonstrates that, at the highest level of Yoga, what we do on the outside of ourselves and what we do on the inside are virtually the same. When one is deeply absorbed in meditation on the inside (as in *dharana, dhyana* and *samadhi*), this will certainly be reflected in one's conduct on the outside (as in *yama, niyama* and *asana*). And when a yogi is absorbed in *samadhi*, he or she attains at the deepest level of *samadhi* what Patanjali calls *dharma-megha-samadhi*. One becomes completely absorbed by *dharma*, which refers both to personal virtues affecting the outside world and to one's very nature and essence of being. Are we not all pilgrims who can model our inward journey of Yoga after Sri Swamiji's glorious outer journey to Mount Kailash?

Here is a Yoga master who delved deeply into his own tradition, who plunged into the depths of his own path, who would eventually reveal the breadth of all faiths in his groundbreaking interfaith work. He went to the heights of his own tradition so that he could fully experience the connection between all faiths. In this sense, the powerful archetypal symbol of the mountain can be appreciated:

Can we reach the peak of our own path, as Swami Satchidananda did at Mount Kailash? Can we understand the highest point of the teachings of a particular tradition in order to grasp the fullness and richness of the whole of the teaching?

In the *Bhagavad Gita*, Krishna's very last words to his beloved Arjuna engage the symbolic imagery of a mountain: Krishna inquires from Arjuna, "Has this teaching been heard by you, O Arjuna, with thought focused upon the single highest point?" (18.72). Here Krishna implies that the whole of the teaching is likened unto the base of a mountain, and the single highest point (*ekagra*) of the teaching is likened unto a mountain peak. Krishna hopes that Arjuna will view the teachings that have been imparted to him from the highest point of those teachings. To continue with the analogy, we can see all parts of a mountain from its peak. But if we scale a mountain only on one side without reaching the pinnacle, we remain blind to the other sides; we cannot see the whole of the mountain, nor can we see surrounding mountains and peaks. Analogously, when it comes to spiritual knowledge, we remain myopic with respect to the loftiest teachings. Swami Satchidananda teaches, by his example and through his pilgrimage and devotion to Mount Kailash, that we must reach that highest point, that deepest heart of the tradition, for only then comes the dawning of Self-realization.

In his journal, Sri Swamiji acknowledges the mountains and peaks that surround Mount Kailash, sometimes alluding to their symbolic significance. How absurd would it be if Sri Swamiji were to see Mount Kailash as the only mountain in the whole range of the Himalayas? Part of Swami Satchidananda's life work was to convey the interconnection between the diverse spiritual and religious traditions of the world. He was without doubt one of the world's most ardent and effective proponents of interreligious dialogue, and we witness his vision expanding during the journey to Mount Kailash.

Swami Satchidananda beautifully exemplifies, in this journal and in his life, how we must leave the outer world to undertake the pilgrimage–to go deep within ourselves to the innermost center of the heart–and, then, to come back out in order to make a difference in a world of great need. Let us, you and I, follow in the footsteps of Sri Swami Satchidananda by treading the sacred path of Yoga.

–Graham M. Schweig, Ph.D.
Author-translator of *Dance of Divine Love* and *Bhagavad Gita*
Director of The Secret Yoga Institute
April, 2010

Acknowledgements

This book is the happy outcome of a long series of Tamil lectures, interviews, broadcasts and articles that occurred when I returned from Kailash. It arose through the encouragement and cooperation of a great number of the Lord's devotees in Sri Lanka.

Special mention must be made of Mr. K. P. Haran, Editor of the daily newspaper *Ela Nadu*, Mr. Thiyagarajah of (then) Radio Ceylon and of Mr. Paramahamsadhasan, who kindly contributed the reviews.

The Editors of *Sunthanthiran*, Mr. S. T. Sivanayagam and Mr. K. K. Ratnasingham, serialized the account in their weekly newspaper. The book was also printed on their press.

My devoted disciple, S. Lakshmi, patiently edited the manuscript not once, but three times. And now the English translation, so kindly rendered by the painstaking efforts of Mr. P. Shanmugam, has also been published.

My humble and heartfelt thanks and blessings are due them all, as well as the many others who contributed to this work in both large and small ways.

Above all these, my holy benevolent master, His Holiness Sri Swami Sivanandaji Maharaj, has imbued this publication with special greatness by giving it his blessings. I offer my prostrations at his golden feet.

I am ever grateful to the Lord of Kailash for giving me this opportunity to serve His loving children.

Swami Satchidananda

Introduction

Mt. Kailash: Land of the Gods

There is no place more powerful for practice, more blessed or more marvelous than this. May all pilgrims and practitioners be welcome!

–Milarepa, Tibetan Buddhist Yogi (circa 1052–1136)

Tibet is a magical, mysterious land with thrilling landscapes that conjure up images of supernatural beings and thoughts of immortality. The breathtaking Himalayan peaks that ring the enormous Tibetan plateau are the tallest in the world. And from the highest point of this plateau soars Mt. Kailash. According to the *Puranas*, India's vast treasury of literary and spiritual knowledge, Mt. Kailash is the center of the world and its four faces are composed of crystal, ruby, gold and lapis lazuli (*Kailasa* means "crystal" in Sanskrit). Is it any wonder that this dazzling pyramid of ice and snow invokes the fabled utopian world of Shangri-La?

Sacred to four faiths–Buddhism, Jainism, Bon (the pre-Buddhist Tibetan religion) and Hinduism–Mt. Kailash has, for centuries, been a focal point, a spiritual magnet, so to speak, attracting countless pilgrims who sacrifice comfort and safety, sometimes even their very lives, for the sake of expressing their devotion and absorbing the divine energy that permeates this spectacular abode of the gods.

Tantric Buddhists believe that Kailash is the home of Buddha Demchok, who represents Supreme Bliss. Moreover, tradition says that the great yogi, Milarepa, championed Tantric Buddhism and that he came to Tibet to challenge Naro Bon-chung, who promoted the Bon religion. The two sorcerers engaged in a fierce and terrifying magical battle, but they were so well matched that neither could gain a significant advantage over the other. Finally, they agreed to a contest. They would race to the top of Mt. Kailash, and whoever reached the summit first would be the victor. Immediately, Naro Bon-chung sat down on a magic drum and soared up the mountain slope. Meanwhile, Milarepa sat down and remained perfectly still in meditation. His disciples were taken aback, dumbfounded. But when Naro Bon-chung nearly reached the top, Milarepa suddenly leaped into action and overtook him by riding on the rays of the sun, thereby winning the contest. Milarepa, however, grabbed a handful of snow and flung it onto the peak of a nearby mountain, known since as Bonri, bestowing it to the Bonpo and ensuring their link to the region.

The Jains call Mt. Kailash Mt. Ashtapada. Their tradition has it that the founder of their faith, Rishabhadeva, attained *moksha*, or spiritual liberation at Kailash. The Sikhs say that Guru Nank Dev, the founder of Sikhism, is one of the few people believed to have ascended to the summit of Kailash. And Hindus revere Mt. Kailash as the home of Lord Siva, the Lord of Yoga, the Lord of Lords, the Supreme Being, his consort Parvati and their sons, Skanda and Ganesh.

According to Hindu tradition, Lord Siva suffered inconsolably after the death of his beloved first wife, Sati. Grief-stricken, he turned his back on the world and all its pleasures, banishing himself to a dark cave in the Himalayas. Devoting all his time to meditation, Siva gained immense wisdom and spiritual powers. However, having committed himself to a purely ascetic life, he no longer defended the gods against the powerful demons of the underworld who had driven them out of their heavenly homes. Desperate, the gods called upon Mother Goddess Shakti, who suggested that only a son of Siva could wage a successful war against the demons. To this end, Shakti agreed to take another form in order to draw Siva out of his cave and get him to father a warrior son who could vanquish the demons. Thus, Shakti (the feminine principle of the universe) was reborn as the daughter of Himavan, the Lord of the Mountains, and she was called Parvati.

Parvati, the dark-skinned Daughter of the Mountains, loved Siva even when she was a young girl, and she was determined to win his heart and to become his consort. She grew up to be a stunningly beautiful woman, and every day she visited Siva's cave. She swept the floor, decorated it with flowers and offered Siva fruits and other earthly gifts, hoping to lure him out of his meditative state. But, alas, Siva didn't open his eyes. In fact, he never even noticed that she was there. Aware that Siva had vowed never to marry again, Parvati realized that she would have to take drastic measures if she hoped to woo him from his life of solitude and austerity. She enlisted the help of Priti and Rati, the goddesses of love and longing. And with their help, Parvati transformed Siva's cave into a sensuous pleasure garden filled with exotic songbirds, melodious honeybees and the most fragrant flowers. Into this enchanting setting, Kama, the beautiful God of Love, appeared, and he shot Siva with the arrow of desire. But Siva, not amused, simply opened his third eye and blasted Kama with an energy beam that incinerated him on the spot. Thus it was that Love was lost to the world.

The gods were devastated. But Parvati promised: "Don't worry. Siva will become my consort; and, when he does, Kama will be reborn."

With this goal in mind, Parvati disappeared into the forest. There, she became an ascetic, dedicating herself to a life of meditation and the most rigorous austerities: eating almost nothing, exposing her unclothed body to ice, snow and chilling winds in winter, sitting amidst bonfires on the hottest days of summer, and standing motionless on one leg for long periods of time. Totally detaching herself from the world, she gained complete mastery over her body and mind. Parvati became the perfect ascetic, fully matching Siva.

Finally, the *tapas* (heat) generated from Parvati's austerities shook Siva out of his meditative state. He stepped out of his cave, and when he learned of Parvati's achievements, he agreed to become her consort.

Parvati and Siva took part in the most splendid wedding celebrations and then left together for Mt. Kailash. There, the two became one. And from this union, a son, Skanda (the destroyer of demon Taraka), was born, and *Kama*–Love–was restored to the world. Inspired by Parvati's intelligence and beauty, Siva became the source of the arts, dance and drama. The two deities also spent time in deep conversation, questioning each other with respect to the most profound philosophical issues. These conversations became the basis of the *Vedas,* the *Yoga Sutras* and the *Tantras,* sacred texts that are the foundations of the Hindu faith.

Overall, the account of Parvati's efforts to unite with Siva serves as an allegory of the spiritual seeker's quest to merge with the Divine and of the harmony that ensues when one achieves that goal.

Reluctantly, you return…By the same route which took you to the region of immortal joy, the holy Kailash, you re-enter the land of endless suffering, disharmony and misery.

–H. H. Sri Swami Sivanandaji Maharaj

The *Rig Veda*, an ancient Hindu scripture, refers to the Himalayan range as a deity. According to that marvelous Indian epic, the *Mahabharata*, Yudhishtra, the eldest of the five Pandava brothers, ascended the Himalayan peaks in order to reach heaven. Tradition holds that even a single circumambulation around Mount Kailash wipes away the sins of a lifetime. What's more, the *Skanda Purana* declares that one can become free of all sins just by merely looking at the Himalayas. And in *The Way of the White Clouds*, Lama Anagarika Govinda writes: "He who performs the *Parikrama*, the ritual circumambulation of the holy mountain, with a perfectly devoted and concentrated mind, goes through a full cycle of life and death."

In 1930, one such sage, Sri Swami Sivananda, undertook the arduous journey to Mt. Kailash. A medical doctor who became a renunciate, Swami Sivananda had, like Siva and Parvati, practiced many extreme austerities. In Rishikesh, in the Himalayas, he walked the roads with nothing but a cloth around his waist and one over his shoulders, even during the cold winter season. Sometimes, he had nothing to eat for days, drinking only water from the Ganges. He kept himself warm by repeating the name of God with every breath he took. His goal was to achieve enlightenment. And he had such a strong will that he never wavered in the face of temptation, choosing hunger and fatigue over personal comforts, because the gain that he sought was spiritual, not material. It was with this level of determination that he left Swag Ashram, the spiritual community where he had been living and serving, to set off on a pilgrimage to the various sacred Himalayan sites, including Mount Kailash.

He began his pilgrimage to Kailash on June 12, 1930. After an arduous trek, he and the members of his group reached Lake Manasarovar, which lies at the foot of Mt. Kailash. He took a dip in the clear blue waters of the lake before continuing the trek to Kailash, where he walked around the sacred mountain. Before returning to camp, the group set off to Gowri Kund, a lake situated 18,000 above sea level. Here the air was so rarified that it was difficult to breathe. Everyone felt exhausted, but Swami Sivananda broke the ice on the lake's surface and bathed in the freezing water. By the time he arrived at the camp, his face had become blackened by the brutally cold wind and the burning sun, and he had lost fifteen pounds. To him, though, the entire journey had been delightful. In fact, drawing on his medical training and experience, he had served patients and saved lives along the way. Twenty-eight years later, one of his many ardent disciples, the author of this journal, set off on his own pilgrimage to Mt. Kailash, fulfilling a childhood aspiration to visit the abode of the gods.

You go on a pilgrimage to realize that you are nothing and that without God's help you cannot do anything.

–Sri Swami Satchidananda

A world-renowned spiritual teacher, promoter of interfaith harmony and global peace, Sri Swami Satchidananda was born Ramaswamy (Ramu) Gounder in Chettipalayam, a small village in the South Indian state of Tamil Nadu. Ramu grew up in a deeply spiritual environment, absorbing the teachings and witnessing the lifestyle of the wandering *sadhus*, ascetic holy people, and the *sannyasins* (renunciates) who were welcomed and served at his home. He experienced the life of a student, a businessman and a householder. After only a few years of marriage, he lost his wife. It was at this time that Ramu's thoughts turned away from worldly matters. He became interested in the study and practice of Hatha Yoga, focusing especially on three books of Yoga postures, two by Tamil writers and one by Sri Swami Sivanandaji. Before long, he entrusted his two small sons to the care of his family and embarked on a full-time spiritual quest.

Ramu lived in a room in his parents' house, devoting himself entirely to religious studies and meditation. He became more and more introspective. He also grew sensitive to the sounds of daily life that echoed through the house, so he asked his father for permission to build a little place for himself in a lovely flower garden located on family land a mile and a half away. A small hut was constructed, and Ramu secluded himself in his new home, planting and tending a small flower garden so that he would have flowers for his morning *puja* (worship service). He spent the rest of his day meditating and studying the teachings of the great sages and renunciates, including Sri Bhagavan Ramakrishna, Saint Ramalingam, Sri Swami Vivekananda, and Sri Swami Sivananda.

He practiced Hatha Yoga to keep his body fit, and he maintained an austere diet that was limited to one meal a day. Ramu continued this regimen for about a year, and it was in this little garden hut, during deep meditation, that he first revealed his spiritual experiences. Concentrating on his beloved deity, Parvati, Ramu suddenly felt the room aglow with light, filled with the presence of the goddess. Ramu continued to have such visions while meditating in the hut. After some time, although he appreciated the privacy of the little shelter and the opportunity to focus on spiritual study, Ramu felt a yearning to explore spiritual life outside the parameters of his home. And so he began the next phase of his spiritual journey.

In 1945, Ramu left on a pilgrimage to seek out the great South Indian yogis, saints and sages whose timeless teachings were grounded in India's ancient spiritual and philosophical traditions. He spent time among spiritual luminaries such as Sri Sadhu Swamigal, Sri Swami Badagara Sivananda, Sri Swami Ranga Nath, each one a great *siddha* ("an accomplished one," often with psychic powers).

In 1946, Ramu went to the Ramakrishna Mission. There he served at the ashram, staying for some time with Sri Swami Chidbhavanandaji Maharaj. And it was from Swami Chidbhavanandaji that Ramu received *brahmacharya diksha*, initiation into pre-monastic life, and a new name: Sambasivam Chaitanya. *Sambasivam* represents the true harmonizing of the individual soul with the Divine. *Amba* is a name of the goddess Shakti, the cosmic energy; Siva is a name of the cosmic consciousness; and *Chaitanya* means "absolute consciousness." Around this time, Sambasivam also visited Anandashram frequently, sitting at the feet of the all-blissful Swami (Papa) Ramdas and the beloved Mother Krishnabai.

From 1947 to 1948, he traveled around South India as a wandering mendicant. At Aurobindo Ashram in Pondicherry, he received the blessings of the yogi-poet-philosopher-educator Sri Aurobindo and his foremost disciple, the Mother. Continuing his pilgrimage through South India, Sambasivam found his way to Arunachala, spending time with the celebrated *jivanmukta* (living liberated being) Sri Ramana Maharshi. Fourteen days before this renowned sage passed away, Sambasivam left the ashram to resume his pilgrimage. This time, he headed north to Rishikesh, to Sri Swami Sivananda's ashram on the bank of the Ganges.

Actually, even before being initiated into the pre-monastic life, Sambasivam had felt drawn to Rishikesh, a town in the Himalayan hills and home, for centuries, to many saints and sages. For years, he had heard about the illustrious sage, Sri Swami Sivananda Maharaj, who was often called *Jagatguru* (the Great World Guru), as well as Swami Givananda, because of his generous nature. For a long time, Sambasivam experienced a deep desire to receive Master Sivananda's *darshan* (vision or experience of a divine form or being). Finally, in the spring of 1949, he made his way to Rishikesh and to Ananda Kutir, Master Sivananda's ashram.

Life itself is a journey toward Godhead, a pilgrimage.

–Sri Swami Satchidananda

At Ananda Kutir, Sambasivam felt, without a doubt, that he had reached his final destination. He realized that Master Sivananda was his *Satguru*–a spiritual preceptor of the highest attainment, one who has realized the ultimate Truth. Sambasivam was ready to receive *sannyas* initiation, and he knew, unquestionably, that his initiation as a full renunciate would be through the hand of his beloved Guru, Master Sivananda.

Traditionally, before the actual *sannyas* initiation, the aspirant undertakes a pilgrimage for purification. Sambasivam chose as his destination the holy shrines of Kedarnath, Tunganath and Badrinath, three holy places high up in the mountains near Rishikesh. He began the 28-day pilgrimage in May of 1949. This was Sambasivam's first real trekking experience, and he was so inspired by the beauty of the Himalayan region that he stopped periodically to write poems about his journey and songs like this one:

Beloved friend, come on. There is so much beauty,
so much to see at the silver peaks of the Himalayas.
It is a feast for the eyes. Do you know who prepared
that big feast? It is all God....Do you see where the
Ganges is going? It is running toward the Mother
from whom it came, the sea. All these little branches
that join the Ganges are all little seekers. The big
guru (the Ganges) runs toward the Mother, and all
the little seekers join and say, "We will follow you
because we know you are going to take us there."

When he returned to the ashram, Sambasivam continued his service, teaching Hatha Yoga classes and answering correspondence in the South Indian Tamil language; later on, he gave Raja Yoga lectures at the Yoga Vedanta Forest Academy, the school attached to the ashram. A couple of months later, on July 10, a warm, clear day, Sambasivan presented himself to his guru, ready for initiation into the holy order of *sannyas*. With his head and face freshly shaved, as tradition prescribes, Sambasivam sat before the sacrificial fire as thousands of *sannyasins* had done before him. He symbolically offered up his body, mind, intellect and all worldly attachments. Then, standing in the holy river Ganges, he repeated the *Mahavakyas* ("Great Sayings" of the *Upanishads*), and he received the *sannyas mantra* (sacred sound vibration) for the first time. He dipped into the water three times and then accepted the traditional orange cloth of renunciation from his Guru. He now shed the name that he had been given as a pre-*sannyasin* and received the new name and title chosen by his Guru. Sambasivam was given the Sanskrit title of "Swami," or "master of one's own self," and the name Satchidananda, which means "Truth-Knowledge-Bliss Absolute."

While he lived at Ananda Ashram, Swami Satchidananda frequently visited Vasishta Guha (Vasishta's Cave), which was located some fourteen miles in the hills above the ashram. This cave was perfect for meditation and was inhabited by a contemporary of Master Sivananda, Swami Purushottamanandaji Maharaj. In his search for a secluded place to meditate, Swami Purushottamanandaji had settled in the Guha. He used to sit outside on a small platform to talk with Swami Satchidananda; the latter visited so often that the two became quite close. After listening to the inspiring *satsang* (spiritual discussion), Swami Satchidananda would ask for permission to go inside the cave to meditate. And, as recounted in his biography, *Sri Swami Satchidananda: Apostle of Peace*, it was here that he described the following spiritual experience:

> *My highest experience, not connected with any particular form, was the experience of Adwaita, or Oneness or Enlightenment. I had that experience in 1949, a few months after my sannyas initiation. It was in midwinter when I visited Vasishta Cave. Vasishta was a great rishi, a sage who lived hundreds of years ago. There is a legend that it was in this cave that he performed his austerities.*

> *I went into the cave, bending down, until after twenty-five feet, I reached a large room-like place with a seat. As I sat there and meditated, I had the experience of transcending my body and mind, realizing myself as the*

Omnipresent. I forgot my individuality. It is impossible to explain exactly what this is.

I must have spent several hours in that state. Then I heard a humming sound, OM chanting, coming from a long distance away. Slowly, slowly, it became louder. As it neared, I became aware of my mind and body. Gently, I stood up and went out of the cave.

For some time, I couldn't see anything in the normal way. All over I saw light, light, light. The whole world appeared to be a mass of light. There was only peace everywhere. The state persisted that whole day.

Of course, after that I had this experience very often, mostly when I visited a holy place. I had it in Badrinath and almost every day when I went to Mount Kailash. I had it in Amarnath in Kashmir. Even in Sri Lanka, whenever I visited Adam's Peak. I had it in Jerusalem and at St. Peter's in the Vatican.

In the spiritual life, all paths lead to the same place.

–Sri Swami Satchidananda

By 1952, Swami Satchidananda had been living at Sivananda Ashram for almost three years. Seekers who came to the ashram and those whom he served in other places recognized him as a great yogi and healer, some of them becoming devotees who acknowledged him as their Guru. During the year, a female *sannyasin* from Ceylon (presently, Sri Lanka), who was also named Swami Satchidananda and who belonged to the Tamil-speaking community, asked Master Sivananda for permission to open a branch of the Divine Life Society in her home country. She also asked that the other Swami Satchidananda accompany her to help start up the organization. The other Swami Satchidananda, however, had no desire to leave Rishikesh; all he wanted was to continue living and meditating in the seclusion of the ashram. While the female Satchidananda was aware that her counterpart was reluctant to leave the ashram, she also knew that he was an excellent teacher and that he spoke Tamil.

Unbeknown to Swami Satchidananda from the little village of Chettipalayam, the wheels of change–and destiny–had been set in motion and his life would be taking a new and, at least to him, surprising turn. Soon, he was approached by Master Sivananda, who announced the Ceylonese Swami's request. Thinking, maybe hoping, that a refusal would end the matter, the modest disciple declared that he was not fit to do such work and that he was content to continue with the work that he was already doing. To further his argument, he also maintained that two Swamis with the same name would obviously cause confusion. But Master Sivananda saw the whole picture–and he knew all the solutions. First he said, "Go ahead. I will work through you. Don't worry." Then he laughed and said, "From now on, she will be known as Swami Satchidananda Mataji (Mother) and you can use Yogiraj–the title I gave you [meaning Yoga Master]. You will be known as Yogiraj Swami Satchidananda."

So, the next chapter of Yogiraj Satchidanandaji's life was about to begin. Never again would he lead a life of seclusion. Instead, his dedicated service to humanity and his mission to disseminate the teachings of Yoga and to promote interfaith harmony and world peace would propel him across oceans and continents for as long as he remained in the physical body.

He arrived in Ceylon on February 1, 1953, and the new ashram was dedicated on the 7th of November. Soon afterwards, construction began on an orphanage and free medical dispensary. The center also created cottage industries where unemployed girls and young women were employed to do hand weaving. These women and girls came from many communities: they were Hindus, Buddhists, Muslims and Christians. The precepts that Swami Satchidananda taught were: "Serve and Love" and "Truth is one, paths are many." Many people from diverse backgrounds came to the ashram, drawn to the loving kindness and exemplary life of Yogiraj Satchidananda. They came for advice and to study and practice Yoga. Many of those spiritual seekers acknowledged him as their Guru, calling him Gurudev, the endearing term that disciples use when speaking or referring to their spiritual preceptors.

His own Gurudev, Master Sivanandaji, was so pleased with his disciple's service that he wrote to him from Rishikesh:

Your radiant personality and spiritual aura attract people to you; and your genuine humility and eagerness to serve all earn their admiration and affection. The newspaper reports reveal that your inspiring discourses command great respect and lead the men and women of Ceylon along the path of selflessness, unity and dynamic service to the goal of peace and prosperity. I pray to the Lord to confer upon you continued radiant health and long life!

May God bless you.
Victory to the Divine!

After five years at the ashram in Ceylon, Gurudev decided to make a pilgrimage to holy Mt. Kailash, the legendary home of his *Ishta Devata* (personal form of God), Lord Siva. He undertook this journey with Sri Swami Premanandaji of Poona, Sri Swami Bagawathanandaji of the Himalayas, Sri Praveen Nanawati of Bombay and Sri Ramdas of Punjab. The pilgrimage took two months.

The entire journey is described in this book, a day-by-day personal account of an extraordinary adventure and an unforgettable spiritual experience. In his journal, Sri Gurudev vividly describes the stunning beauty of the mountains, valleys and lakes; the robust and accommodating indigenous people; the mystical atmosphere; and the challenges and perils that are inescapable in such an undertaking. His clear language and detailed descriptions will have you riveted to your seat as you follow him on the trek, by foot, through 800 miles of rocky and dangerous ascents and descents that will take him to a height of 19,000 feet.

You will hold your breath as you picture in your mind's eye the mules, laden with baggage, struggling through the deep snow, then toppling over; the treacherous descents on slippery slopes that could, and sometimes do, end in death; the night that the mules and their keepers got separated from the group, leaving the pilgrims stranded in the piercing cold wind without food, tents or bedding; the experience of nearly freezing to death; and the divine spirit that guided Gurudev back to life.

To be sure, you, too, are about to embark on a sacred pilgrimage. For, as Sri Patanjali tells us in his *Yoga Sutras*, immersion in the lives of the saints and sages inspires us to climb to greater heights. And, while Gurudev physically scaled enormous heights, endured freezing temperatures and hazardous terrain and faced death itself in order to reach Mt. Kailash, the center of the world and abode of the gods, his journey is most meaningful in that it symbolizes the inner journey upon which all human beings, knowingly or unknowingly, are embarked. For all those qualities that are indispensable to one who sets out on a pilgrimage to a place like Mt. Kailash—endurance, courage, perseverance, commitment, discipline, confidence, flexibility and the faith in oneself and in a Higher Power—are just as indispensable to the spiritual seeker undertaking his or her own inner pilgrimage, the journey to the Divine center within us.

Indeed, the notion of the *axis mundi*, the center of the world, where the upper and lower realms conjoin, where the feminine and masculine principles merge, crosses all cultural boundaries. We project this archetype onto exalted sites that elevate us, literally and figuratively, above the mundane existence of our daily lives. But, in reality, the true center of the universe—with all its marvels and miracles—lies within us. The pure bliss of that realm can be found in the depths of our own psyche, that sacred place where Cosmic Consciousness (Siva) and its manifestation (Parvati) reside in unity.

So, as we absorb ourselves in the thrilling experiences that Sri Gurudev chronicled in his *Kailash Journal*, let's keep in mind an observation made by the late historian of religion, Mircea Eliade: "Every microcosm, every inhabited region has a centre, that is to say, a place that is sacred above all." And that includes us.

–Reverend Kumari DeSachy, Ed.D.
Integral Yoga Ministry
Author, *Bound to Be Free*
April, 2010

View of the author en route.

Chapter 1

Pilgrimage

Everyone likes to go on a journey, but for the spiritual seeker a journey is an essential part of worship and therefore a special joy. Since ancient times, followers of various faiths have traveled long distances on pilgrimage in search of the Lord. Bethlehem is the place of pilgrimage revered by Christians. Followers of Islam consider travel to Mecca to be the holiest of acts. Buddhists find great solace in going to such places as Buddha Gaya and Saranath. A visit to the Holy Land of Israel is cherished by Jewish people. There are a number of places of pilgrimage revered by the Hindus; Mount Kailash stands high among these in greatness.

The pilgrimage to a holy place in search of the Lord is a short journey taken only by a few. The journey which all souls take–through birth, life, death and the final joy of becoming one with the Lord–is a very long one. Each soul is given a physical body to serve as its vehicle. As it travels through this world, it undergoes a great variety of experiences. If the soul has not reached its destination–and the pilgrimage remains unfinished–by the time its vehicle wears out, it acquires another vehicle in another birth and continues the journey. There is no doubt that ultimately the soul will become one with the Lord, even if it takes millions and billions of births to achieve. There are many, many experiences of pleasure and pain to be encountered along the way. However, even the painful experiences can be a joy if we understand the nature of this life. It is very much like an obstacle race.

The Obstacle Race

We are all familiar with the obstacle race. High bars, low bars, fences, tunnels, ditches, rings and pits all stand between the starting post and the finish line. Of course it would be easy to go around the obstacles, but the object of the race is to complete the course by going over them. The participants will have to jump, climb, crawl or leap over each hurdle in order to finish the race. The one who comes in first will be awarded the winner's cup; prizes will be given to those coming in second and third. A few certificates might also be given out, but the majority of the participants will go home without any award.

The obstacle race conducted by Him, our Lord, has a unique characteristic. There are many, many participants in this game of life, but all of them will be rewarded. The award is His cup of grace, and it is given to all—whether first, last or in between. The Lord keeps calling: "Come one and all. To every one who comes I shall award my cup of grace."

How He loves His children! He wants them all to get prizes. At the same time, it is not reasonable to give prizes to those who do not participate. Therefore, He makes everyone participate and awards everyone His grace. If anyone tries to avoid playing the game, the Lord will simply put obstacles in his way and make him play. If we understand this well, we will see His hand at work when obstacles appear before us, and knowing what is to be gained, we will boldly face them.

A pilgrimage is also like an obstacle race. Through the obstacles the seeker expands into divine consciousness and comes to understand the game of life. The very purpose of the pilgrimage is to obtain that grace. Traversing rugged paths, crossing mountains, rivers and jungles, facing cold, hunger and sleepless nights, undeterred by misfortune, discomfort or danger, thinking only of the Lord day and night, pursuing but one goal above all else—enduring all this the pilgrim becomes a noble traveler. He comes to realize that he eats, sleeps and acts only by the will of God and not by his own will. He learns that his very breath is "his" by virtue of that grace alone. He vows to be ever mindful of the Lord's grace—at all times, in all conditions—and dedicates his body, mind, soul and every possession to God. This dedication removes the obstacles of "I" and "mine" that stand between every earnest seeker and God.

Departure to Kailash

As previously mentioned, Hindus make pilgrimages to many places. Pilgrimage to Kailash is the most difficult of all. Some people believe that it is impossible for mere mortals to ascend Mount Kailash, and in olden times there were very few who would even consider such a pilgrimage. Travel facilities did not exist in those days. The entire journey across hills, rivers and thick jungles had to be made on foot. Accidents were commonplace. The pilgrim had to drink from streams and live on herbs and fruits found in the jungle. Very few of those who undertook this journey lived to return. It is for this reason that death is commonly referred to as "departure to Kailash."

You might wonder why anyone would undertake such a journey at the risk of his very life. It is true that the journey is one of extreme difficulty, but the pilgrim to Mount Kailash achieves that rare and privileged experience of seeing God appear before him in the very forms of nature. This vision brings boundless joy and reveals great spiritual truths about the nature of life itself.

The Truths Revealed There

Mount Kailash is flanked on one side by Manasa Sarovaram, a clear, calm lake, and on the other by Rakshas Taal. Manasa Sarovaram means "lake like a peaceful mind." Rakshas Taal means "Demon Lake" or "lake like a *rajasic* mind." This lake is rippled with dark, muddy waves. The pure, untainted Absolute is clearly present in Mount Kailash, which stands tall and majestic between the two lakes of opposite nature, totally unaffected by the nature of either. However, its image, which is reflected in the waters of the calm Manasa Sarovaram, cannot be seen at all in the cloudy waters of the Demon Lake.

If we look deeply into ourselves, we can see how much the mind of the individual is like a lake. It is clear and calm when possessed of pure thoughts, and cloudy when rippled with disturbing thoughts. The soul, which is free of all thought, is like Mount Kailash; it simply radiates that pure nature of the omnipresent Absolute. However, just as the image of Kailash can only be seen in the calm lake, this image of God can only be reflected by the pure, untainted mind and heart. It is the very rigors of the pilgrimage that purify the mind and heart and enable the individual to realize the presence of God and to reflect His image.

Swami Premanandaji Maharaj with author. He was the one mainly responsible for inspiring and organizing the pilgrimage.

Chapter 2

The Decision to Go

The decision to make this pilgrimage was not a sudden whim. The name of the Lord–the One who is both father and mother to all souls and who continually blesses His children–had been familiar to me even as a young child. When I later heard of His holy abode in the pristine panorama of Kailash, the desire to pay Him homage in this holy setting was kindled. That spark remained aglow for many years.

On the evening of 19 December 1957, I was sitting on the banks of the Mahaweli Ganga, the longest river in Sri Lanka, with Swami Premanandaji, who was visiting from India at the time. Our minds were filled with peace and calm in the serene twilight, and our conversation naturally centered on the great blessings of God. Both of us agreed that the treasures of nature reflect His grace, and, if that is so, then Mount Kailash stands foremost among all the gems of the Himalayas. Discovering that we had the same thirst to drink the divine nectar of His blessings at Kailash, we resolved then and there to make the pilgrimage. Swami Premanandaji offered to make the necessary arrangements from Bombay. Since the months of June, July and August are best suited to this journey, we thought it prudent to wait until then.

The following April, I received a letter from Swamiji informing me that the preparations were under way and requesting that I set a date to come to India. I wrote back that I would arrive in Bombay on the 20th of May and began to get myself ready. I obtained what supplies I could in Colombo and Kandy, and planned those purchases that would have to be made when I reached India. The pilgrim to Kailash must take food and provisions for two months, and clothing and bedding heavy enough to face the ice and snow. Camping equipment is also essential: you will not find any hotels or restaurants on the peaks.

Top: Trisuli Peak: The Himalayas abound with both beauty and danger for the pilgrim.
Below: Accommodation in the hills.

It Will Not Be Possible to Dine as Usual

The pilgrim should be ready to give up his customary food. It is not possible to cook many of our usual foods at the high altitudes in the Tibetan region of the Himalayas, and most of them do not grow there anyway. Flat breads, such as *puri* and *chapathi*, will be the main diet, since wheat flour is the most prevalent staple in the hills. At the beginning of the journey, potatoes and onions will be available, but you will not even have these later on. Dried vegetables, pickles and other canned and non-perishable foods should be taken, as well as condensed milk, coffee, tea and sugar. Cooking utensils will be needed; aluminum is lightweight and heats quickly, but a pressure cooker is actually most ideal for cooking at the higher elevations. When you stop to eat or sleep, you will find neither fireplace nor firewood; therefore it is absolutely essential to take a kerosene stove. A thermos bottle will also prove very handy.

Woolens—gloves, bedsheets, blankets and clothing—should be taken to protect oneself from the icy Himalayan cold. A good sleeping bag is the best safeguard overnight when the temperature drops sharply. Sturdy ankle boots and a spiked staff are essential for climbing the steep, snow-covered slopes. You will also need an umbrella for the sudden heavy rains. Until you are actually out on the slopes, however, you will not fully appreciate the lifesaving importance of being properly equipped.

More Hints

Mules and porters must be hired for transporting the two-month supply of food, provisions and equipment. A pocket scale will be very useful in determining the weight of the load while bargaining with porters, and might also save quite a bit of time when disputes arise. Mules can be hired for riding as well, but one should be prepared to fall off now and then. Generally speaking, pilgrimage to Kailash is not for the poor and weak; it is best suited to the strong and wealthy. The cost of a reasonably comfortable trip from Almora to the crest of Kailash and back, with adequate provisions, could easily exceed 500 rupees, or about US $100, in 1958; today it would cost twenty times as much, or even more.

Transportation in the hills comes in two varieties: two-legged and four-legged.

Since even the healthy and strong are subject to illness and accidents while traveling in the hills, it would be wise to carry any medicines that might be needed for the most common ailments and injuries. In addition to all of this, one should pack such personal items as notebook, pen, pencil, needle, thread, knife and flashlight. Remember, as you go higher and higher up into the hills, you will not be able to buy even the simplest of articles. Those interested in photography should be sure to take plenty of film and all necessary equipment. A pair of binoculars would also be handy. Dark glasses are essential to protect your eyes from the blinding glare of the brilliant white snow.

To Ensure Success

While on the slopes, it will be wise to boil all drinking water, no matter what its source. After a few days of acclimation, you may—if you desire—drink unboiled clean water, but only if it comes from clear natural springs. If you drink unboiled water from the rivulets of melting snow, its extremely cold temperature will weaken the bowels and cause dysentery.

Make a point of not touching any plants, or eating any leaves or fruits from plants passed along the way. Poisonous herbs bearing the most beautiful fruits grow abundantly along the steep, narrow footpaths. You might find goats and mules coming toward you on the path; if so, get quickly to a place where there is enough room for you to move off to the side along the uphill slope. If you do not remove yourself from the path, you are liable to be knocked over the precipice by the animals and "reach Kailash" in double-quick time.

While ascending the slopes, remember to look ahead; looking back will bring about giddiness and impede the ascent. Try to start each day's journey early in the morning and stop by about three in the afternoon; it is all too easy to get lost in the evening fog. Take every step with firmness. Make every step count. Let your mind be filled with divine thoughts. You will accomplish the pilgrimage with success.

Farewell

Before I left for Kailash, the Lord blessed me with the opportunity to get together with a great many of His devotees in Trincomalee and Kandy. We spent a long time talking and wishing each other well. When the time finally came to say goodbye, they all asked, "When will you return?" This question is ordinarily asked out of politeness or curiosity; but in the case of pilgrimage to Kailash it is an expression of deep concern. They might as well have asked, "Will you return at all?" since that was the question in their minds. I told them, "I am going to Kailash. When the Lord has brought me to His abode, given me His *darshan* (vision) and seen fit to send me back, I shall return." One devotee who was a little bolder than the others pressed the point further. What followed was a very moving exchange that brought to light a great spiritual truth.

He said, "You say that you are going to see your spiritual parents. Don't stay with them forever; come back to your spiritual children." I told him, "If they bid me to return, I will." The devotee said, "Tell the Lord that your children in Sri Lanka need you. You will be able to go to Him again another time." I said, "But the Lord might say, 'If you return, the children will not permit you to come to me again. Stay here, and they will also come here in search of you.'" The devotee said, "We have neither the physical stamina nor the spiritual strength to go to Kailash now. Therefore we will pray that you be sent back to us." "All right. My return is your will, but ultimately it is His will that will be done. He knows what is best for all concerned, and if He sees fit to answer your prayers by sending me back to you, that will be His grace. May your prayers be answered with His all-seeing wisdom." The conversation came to a close and we said goodbye.

On the morning of 15 May 1958, I left Satchidananda Thapovanam in Kandy in the company of a number of devotees who escorted me to the railway station. As the wheels of the train started to roll down the tracks, tears too rolled down some of their cheeks. I watched until they had disappeared from sight, and quite soon afterward realized that I was in Colombo. I was glad to be able to spend some time with the devotees there as well. A group of them saw me off at the airport the following afternoon. As the plane soared, so did my thoughts. The pilgrimage I had dreamed of for so long had really begun!

While the plane flew over the vast expanse of countryside, a colorful kaleidoscope passed below. There were hills, valleys, rivers, lagoons, tall buildings, tiny cottages, giant trees scaling the sky, shrubs and vines embracing the earth. Each had its own particular beauty. This is one of the great lessons of nature. Those who have realized God see no difference between high and low, colors, sizes and shapes. Everything is equal in their eyes, just as all of creation is equally beloved by its Creator.

An Auspicious Delay

The plane landed at Meenambakam Airport, Madras, at 4:30 p.m. I had a two-day layover before boarding the train to Bombay. I had planned to join Sri Swami Premanandaji at Bombay, but he had already left for Delhi to make some preparations there for the trip. I finally met up with him in Delhi on the 23rd, only to find that our departure was to be delayed for a few more days pending the arrival of the rest of our party. Although this seemed to be a setback in our journey, I was very glad to have the opportunity to make a trip to Rishikesh to see my holy Master Sri Swami Sivanandaji Maharaj and obtain his blessings in person for this holy pilgrimage.

The Pilgrims Gather

I returned to Delhi in time to catch the Punjab Mail on the morning of 2nd June for a scheduled meeting in Mathura with Swami Premanandaji and Mr. Praveen Nanawathi of Bombay, who was also making the pilgrimage. Mr. Praveen had brought two welcome additions to our supplies: sleeping bags, which he had rented for us all from the Himalayan Club, and a farewell gift from Lady Thackeray, a leading resident of Bombay who had founded a number of well-known charitable institutions. This kindly lady had sent our group a host of sweet snacks, all suitably packed for traveling. The rest of that day was spent in visiting the holy temples of Mathura and Vrindavan, and we boarded the train to Kathkodam at 11:30 p.m.

When we reached Paroli Junction, we met up with Mr. Ramdas of Punjab who had the food and cooking gear with him. We were also joined by Kunthan Singh, a 14-year-old boy who was a native of the Himalayan Mountains and who served as an aide to Swami Premanandaji during his various other Himalayan trips. He was the fifth and final member of our party. When locomotives had been attached to both the front and the rear of the train, we started our long uphill journey. The train wound its way through the thick jungle and finally puffed into Kathkodam Railway Station at noon the next day, ending its exhausting climb with a noisy sigh of relief.

Rivulets of melted snow from the surface of mountains and glaciers tumble down the rocks and valleys to become the great rivers of India, and eventually to become one with the ocean.

Chapter 3

Bus Ride from Kathkodam

Kathkodam is a small but well-known town. When the passengers disembarked from our train with their baggage, they were surrounded by autos competing for their attention. Even though a full car left the station every few minutes, there was no danger of being left behind; as soon as one left, another pulled up to take its place. Of course, pilgrims to Kailash are very few, and most of the cars were filled with baggage.

Our party boarded the state bus that was ready to leave just as we arrived. It started its climb through the world-renowned Himalayan hills with a heavy burr of its engine. Our hearts, rejoicing over the sight we would soon be having of Kailash, leapt up and up and up over the hills ahead of the bus! The bus ran along smoothly for a while, then suddenly began to groan very deeply. I looked out to find that the vehicle was starting a steep upward climb. Its deep drone emphasized the determination, strength of mind and willingness to undergo any hardship that one needs to ascend toward the higher goals of life.

The View from the Bus

The scenery we viewed from the moving bus was varied and lively. Terraced paddy fields spread out on either side of the road. Innumerable varieties of jungle growth spread even further. The young paddy plants danced in the wind, inviting our minds to dance along with them. Flower-laden trees dotted the roadside greenery with dazzling colors. All of the forms of life seen along the way were artistically arranged by nature into well-composed scenes. A gentle breeze came through the trees and right on into the bus, refreshing the travelers and including them in the picture.

The sun meanwhile was performing magic tricks with its rays, making all of the brilliant colors before us appear luminous. A voice from up front shouted, "Here comes an elbow bend!" I wondered how the bus would maneuver, but before I could blink an eye we had executed a very sharp turn and were once more running smoothly along the straightaway. It seemed that the bus driver knew some magic tricks of his own. As we entered the heart of the hills, the plains and jungles were gradually replaced by other equally beautiful scenes. All of the sights of the Himalayas are astounding in their physical beauty, but they also have a grace and nobility which give evidence to the spiritual side of life. Let us travel ahead with our imagination and take a look at them.

The Himalayan Range

The Himalayan range stands high at the northern border of India, extending from Kashmir in the west to Assam in the east. It is roughly 1,500 miles long and 300 miles wide, and is subdivided into three regions: the Lesser Himalayas, the Greater Himalayas and the Trans Himalayas. Their snow-covered peaks reach high into the sky. Those of greater renown are Everest (29,028 feet), Kanchenjunga (28,146 feet), Dhaulagiri (26,810 feet), Nanga Parvatam (26,660 feet), Nanda Devi (25,645 feet), Kamet (25,447 feet), Kurla Mandhata (25,355 feet), Duranagiri (25,184 feet), the triple peaks of Trisuli (23,406 feet, 22,490 feet and 22,360 feet), Swaragarohini (23, 420 feet) and Kailash (22,028 feet).

The name *Himalayas* comes from the words *himam*, meaning snow, and *aalayam*, meaning temple. There is no place in this world that could surpass this Temple of Snow in natural beauty. These are the highest mountains on earth. They are young and rugged, and their very ruggedness adds to their majesty. Mount Kailash, outstanding in this range, is often called the "King of Mountains." The atmosphere there invokes higher thoughts and bestows spiritual energy to the soul. It is easy to feel the presence of God at home in His creation in such a place, and devotees come from far and wide to pay Him homage here.

Physical Wealth

The route to Kailash is filled with wonder. The valleys are narrow and steep, and the crystal clear streams running through them glisten in the sunlight. From a distance, these mountain streams look like garlands of pearls adorning the chest of the King of Mountains–or perhaps silver threads woven into the shawl covering his broad shoulders. At various points they tumble innocently with a sweet gurgle, crash over boulders in a chilly rage and sweep over the feet of flowering shoreline plants with soft caresses.

The great rivers of India–the Ganges, Yamuna, Sindhu and Brahmaputhra–all have their source here. They crawl over the summit like babies at play, running in zigzag courses for a short distance before cascading down the slopes. The mountain streams and rivulets of melted snow meet them along the way downhill and become absorbed in their flow. The flooded rivers all steadily gain momentum, becoming ever fuller, broader and more powerful until–full-grown–they reach their ultimate destiny and become one with the ocean. These rivers are like the soul, which is always running to become one with the Lord, no matter where its course seems to be taking it.

The high cliffs of the mountain range stand like sentinels. They are steadfast soldiers, unaffected by such dualities of life as pleasure and pain, profit and loss, praise and blame. Pindari, Milam and Gangothri are some of the many glaciers of the Himalayas. Kashmir, Kulu Valley, Jumount, Nepal, Bhutan, Sikkim–all situated here–are regions world-renowned for their natural beauty. The Himalayan hills are rich in gold, iron and other mineral deposits. The herbs growing here have been found to cure many ailments and invigorate the body, and health resorts abound.

Spiritual Wealth

Even more significant are the landmarks where thousands of sages and saints have performed penance. Not only the landmarks, but waves of holy vibrations remain to this day. They pervade the air and elevate the traveler to higher planes. God-consciousness takes the place of I-consciousness. There are great renunciates to be found here yet, and it will always be so. The atmosphere is one of serenity and surrender, where not only people, but animals, plants and the very elements themselves live in contentment. Fragrant flowers in multitudes of colors dazzle the region. Lily-white blossoms welcome the traveler with their delicate smiles. Slender stalks fall at his feet, shed their flowers there and find joy in this offering. Tender vines, unable to stand on their own, entwine the tall trees, reminding the pilgrim that he who surrenders to God and holds Him fast will find strength and joy in His unfailing support.

The trees that gift the pilgrim with their sweet fruits sway gently in the wind, asking for nothing in return. Their lives say something too: "Do not live for yourself. Give all that you have to the world. That will bring you the greatest pleasure." Forests, plains, lakes and shrublands all lend their beauty to the Himalayas. Their special joy must be experienced to be known. The handiwork of the Creator, who sees with the eye of intuitive wisdom, must be seen by our own eyes before we can truly realize His greatness. Amarnath, Gangothri, Yamunothri, Kedarnath, Badrinath and Kailash all contribute to the fame of the Himalayas as important places of pilgrimage where truth–as well as beauty–is evident.

Well, it is time for us to descend from the realm of imagination and enjoy the actual sights as we pass them by.

Chapter 4

Raniket: Even the Pavement is Beautiful

3 June. The path to Kailash is not a continuous climb; instead it goes up and down one small hill after another. Raniket is one of the hill stations found along the way. It lies 52 miles from Kathkodam, at 6,000 feet above sea level. The black tar of the roads, edged with white rubble on either side, gives a special beauty to the countryside. Green pastures, shrubs and vines all grow luxuriantly along the route. The roads here are excellent, and as the bus rounded the bends, we felt as if we were floating over the ground. A fellow traveler pointed out that Raniket is an army camp, and hence the superb condition of the roads. The camp had brought many other modern facilities to this small town as well.

We stopped to rest here for half an hour, and then resumed our eastward journey.

Almora: Popular and Peaceful

Almora is another 36 miles beyond Raniket, at an altitude of 5,500 feet. Here we parted company with the bus and crew that had skillfully transported us across the 88 miles of hills from Kathkodam. The sun was rapidly setting as our weary group sought out a place to spend the night. We took rooms at the Ambassador Hotel and retired after an early dinner.

Almora is a significant town in this area. Pilgrims to Kailash usually break journey here for a few days in order to make arrangements for the rest of their trip. This beautiful and peaceful spot is also a popular health resort. The people who live here have a wealth of kindness and faith in God. Their hospitality is inexhaustible, like the endless pleasure of a song, and they give of it freely. The town is governed by a town council. The schools, colleges, banks, hospitals, courts, jails, forestry department and other offices here serve the people for miles around and add to the town's importance.

The Treasures of Almora

The residents of Almora weave lovely woolen carpets, sold predominately through the government carpet sales establishment. This is a large organization, housed along with other government offices in an old fort dating back to the Chandra dynasty. A number of spiritual organizations are also found here. There is a Ramakrishna Mission center on the slopes of a high mountain, a charitable trust dedicated to Mother Anandamayi and a Christian mission. There is also a society to aid pilgrims that assists them in arranging for the food, clothing and transport mules necessary for their journey.

4 June. We strolled around Almora for a closer look. Brooks and rivulets interlace the entire surroundings. A temple dedicated to Lord Siva, who is also called Viswanathar, the Cosmic Father, is situated on the banks of the Sanval River. We were blessed with a visit to this sacred shrine. A temple dedicated to the Divine Mother, Shakti, who manifests as the power of nature, is also found in this lovely, quiet spot. Here she is known as Nanda Devi, the Ever-Wakeful Mother. She greets her children with her right hand raised in *abhaya mudra*, showing that there is no need to fear, and her left hand stretched out to bless, inviting one and all to take refuge in her and lay their prayers at her feet. Another temple to Shakti is to be found in a beautiful valley in the northern outskirts of Almora; here she is called Patha Devi, the Mother-Within-the-Earth. A short distance from this holy place is a point where a clear, open expanse of sky forms an endless blue backdrop for the silver-colored, snow-clad peaks. Nanda Devi, Trisuli, Kedar, Badri and Neelakandan can be seen among them.

The Streets Of Heaven

We wandered along Brighton Street, enjoying the sights. At the end of the street we came to the Ramakrishna Math, where Swami Aparnanandaji welcomed us warmly. We paused for a moment in the large hall to absorb the holy vibrations, and entered a room filled with peace and sanctity where we offered our prayers before the altar. Every evening during our stay in Almora, we would come to the Ramakrishna Math to hear stories of God read aloud from the *Mahabharata*. The life story of the great teacher Sri Ramanuja was also read, and a lively discussion would follow. As we were leaving, Swami Aparnanandaji kindly gave us his blessings as well as some sweets that had been offered at the altar. Once such food has been offered to God, it becomes sanctified. It is then given to the worshipper as *prasad*, which in turn sanctifies him.

The sun was setting with a bright glow as we returned to the hotel. Darkness quickly spread its wings far and wide. The headlights of the autos winding through the mist-covered hills flashed like lightning. Street lights along the distant highways sparkled like myriads of stars against the black sky. We could hear the sound of boulders thundering down the rivers in the hills. It seemed as if we were in another world, and we wondered if these were not the streets of heaven as we wound our way back to the hotel, totally absorbed in the wonders of Almora.

Firmness is Needed

During our brief stay in Almora, we also met a kind gentleman named Sri Shanthilal Thriveddi. His generosity touched our hearts, and his sound advice gave us a lot to think about. Our conversation centered on travel to Kailash, and many of the stories and descriptions we have previously heard were now made fresh in our minds.

Of all pilgrimages, pilgrimage to Kailash is the most difficult. Kailash lies in Tibet, on the northern border of the Himalayan range. In order to even reach the foot of Kailash, one has to cross the Greater Himalayas. There are no proper paths for the pilgrim towards the north, so it is necessary to take a more roundabout approach. Much of this range is buried in snow that never melts. The paths that do exist can only be attempted during the few warm months; in winter, they too are blocked by snow. It is true that many of the difficulties of travel here have been alleviated by modern land development, and the paths in the hills are improving, gradually, all the time. Even so, pilgrimage to Kailash could scarcely be considered a pleasure trip. One must have firmness of mind and foot, as well as great courage, if one is to face the difficulties of the Himalayas and ascend beyond them.

Many Paths to One Goal

There are a number of routes commonly used by pilgrims to reach Kailash:

1. From Sri Nagar, the capital of Kashmir, through Ladak and Ghartok. This is the longest route.
2. From Tehri-Garhwal.
3. From Simla, through Shipki Pass.
4. From Gangothri, the source of the Ganges, by way of Nilam Pass.
5. Through Badri Narayan and the Mana Pass. This route takes you by Tolingamut, the renowned Tibetan monastery.
6. From Almora through Lippu Lake Pass.
7. From Almora through Milam Glacier and Undathura.

Altogether, the journey to Kailash and back covers approximately 500 miles. All of the paths are equally difficult to climb. The majority of pilgrims take the route leading from Almora through Lippu Lake Pass, since this one is the shortest, and most of them prefer to come back the same way they go. Since we especially wanted to experience the beauty instilled in nature by God's hand, we decided to ascend by the route leading through the Milam Glacier and Undathura Pass; after circling Kailash, we would come back by way of Garbiang and Lippu Lake Pass.

We Get a Guide and a Friend

It was our great good fortune to have Sri Swami Bagawathanandaji as our guide from Almora on. Although he was already advanced in years, he had a strong body and a keen intellect. He excelled as a guide, giving interesting sidelights and hearty encouragement, as well as the necessary instructions, along the way. He also turned out to be a very good friend.

We discussed our food and clothing provisions with Sri Shanthilal Thriveddi, who assisted us in getting some additional items. In the early morning hours of 5 June, we carefully checked our baggage—food, clothing and equipment—and loaded it onto a bus. We said goodbye to Almora, the town that had hosted us with such kindness and delighted us with such beauty, and left for Bhageswaram.

The Mountains Set an Example

The bus rattled along for 22 miles and then halted abruptly. We had already ascended from 5,500 to 6,060 feet and were now at the Kowsani hill station. We were dazzled by the ever-increasing beauty before us as we journeyed. Mother Shakti continuously lifted our minds and hearts with her scenic wonders, and the higher we climbed, the higher our spirits rose.

At this point, two-thirds of the Himalayas had come into view. We got down off the bus and stood in awe in front of the motionless mountains. The atmosphere was filled with their steadfast tranquility, and they seemed to be giving us their blessings to achieve a steady, unwavering mind and know their peace. The narrow path winding gradually up the slopes reminded us that the path to spiritual attainment is also a slow, steady climb. From here we could see for 200 miles with an unobstructed view of the vast blue sky, the snowy peaks and canyons, where closely grown pine trees rose through luminous clouds. Still, our minds were charged and eager to reach Kailash, the crown of the Himalayan range. The bus, too, seemed to be in a hurry and was suddenly ready to go. It rumbled down the hill at the speed of a roller coaster, and we covered 34 miles in no time. This fast downhill run reminded us of something else: that man and his mind descend to lower levels just that quickly.

Almora: members of our party with a government official seeing us off.
From left to right: Swami Bagawathanandaji of Himalaya; our guide, Mr. Ramdas of
Punjab; Mr. Joshi, the government official; Swami Premanandaji, the organizer, from
Poona; Mr. Praveen Nanawathi, from Bombay; the author, coming from Sri Lanka;
and Sherpas. In front, Kunthan Singh, attendant to Swami Premanandaji.

Chapter 5
Bhageswaram

5 June, Evening. A descent from 6,060 feet to 3,200 feet brought us to Bhageswaram. Here the River Sarayu washes down the hills, forests and rocks, irrigating and enriching the plains as it goes. A rest house on its bank extends the traveler a hearty welcome. The view of the river, with a giant bodhi tree standing on its opposite bank, adds to the lure of the rest house. We spent two wonder-filled days in this place. The point where the holy Gomathi River meets the Sarayu offers a special beauty and a special joy. Pilgrims who bathe here are physically and mentally purified by the holy waters of these rivers.

Markandayar Rock

The evening was peaceful, and the gentle waves of the river extended an invitation of their own. I was in the cool, refreshing water in no time, and soon found my attention drawn to a large rock. I was fascinated by the powerful backlash of the water: it continuously rushed forward and fell backward, showering the rock with its mist. Was the water attempting to pass but retreating in defeat, or simply worshipping the rock by humbly offering it the gift of itself?

A fellow traveler who had noticed me from the shore called out, "That is Markandayar Rock!" I asked him to tell me more. "Markandayar was a great *rishi*. This well-known sage obtained his great wisdom through the power of penance, which he performed while seated on that very rock. During the penance he composed and sang the well-known and much-loved prayer to the Divine Mother, "*Durga Sapthe Sathi*." But the *Puranas* tell that even ages before that, Lord Siva and the daughter of the King of the Himalayas entered into holy matrimony here." I immediately forgot myself and dove into the past. I could almost hear the sacred verses of the *Puranas* echoed in the sounds of the river, telling the story of the union of Siva and Shakti, who pervade the world as Spirit and Nature.

It turned out to be a very long bath; I did not return to the present until the clouds began to darken overhead. The air began to get cooler, and I returned to the rest house. Later that evening we joined the townspeople in chanting *bhajans*. The children participated also, which made the divine words sound even sweeter, and the joyful singing went on for quite a long time. Our tired bones were glad to finally get some rest after dinner.

The Joy of Bhageswaram

The following morning we rose to bathe again at the union of the two holy rivers and then went to the nearby temple. The devotees here celebrate the festival of *Makara Sankaranthi* each year. During these days, the entire population of the area gathers in the town. A temporary supermarket appears for the occasion, offering trade in all sorts of goods. Preparations for the festival are very elaborate, and celebrating all together in this way brings the people to the very brink of joy. We, too, tasted some of that joy when we worshipped at the temple of Siva, the Lord of Bhageswaram.

That afternoon we climbed to the top of the hill in Bhageswaram. This turned out to be a testing ground for the footwear we would be using for the more arduous climbs to follow. This first climb was a short one, and very lovely. There is a temple dedicated to the Divine Mother on the hilltop; here she is known as Chandi, and her presence is strongly felt. After worshipping at her feet, I inquired about the history of the temple. A bystander stepped forward to tell the story, and to praise the greatness of the Holy Mother.

A Buffalo Will Not Substitute for the Ego

One of the things we learned from our impromptu guide was that the people who worshipped Chandi Devi offered buffalos to her as a sacrifice. The buffalo is not very useful to these people, and it viciously attacks anyone who comes across its path. An animal which is that lazy and disagreeable seemed to be a suitable choice for sacrifice.

What the Divine Mother wants is the sacrifice of this lazy mind, which is an obstacle to Self-realization. She wants us to lay the rebellious ego at her altar, not the dead body of an animal. This is the real meaning of "sacrifice." How foolish it is to forget this principle and expect God to be happy with an offering of animals, which are just as much His children as we are.

Ramayana

7 June. A beautiful forest of ashwood decorates the hinterland of Bhageswaram. The supple timber from this species of tree is well-suited for tennis and badminton racquets, and there is a large government factory here that makes them. In Bhageswaram we obtained the spiked staffs needed for climbing the steep, icy hills ahead. That evening we met Mr. Joshi, a college principal who was both well-educated and wise. He was able to speak with us about the trip from his own experience, and we were very grateful for this opportunity to meet with him, since many of the things he had to say were new to us. Later we attended a *satsang*–a spiritual gathering–where the *Ramayana* was read aloud. Hearing the stories of Lord Rama–the dutiful son, brother, husband, warrior and king–on our way to Kailash was an unexpected boon, which we enjoyed immensely.

While in Bhageswaram, we engaged Divan Singh, a cook well-skilled in preparing the kind of food required en route. He turned out to be a sincere friend and faithful servant, as well as an excellent cook.

The Start of the Pilgrimage on Foot

Those unaccustomed to climbing hills cannot carry even the lightest weight on their backs during a trip such as this. Therefore, we hired four mules and two porters to carry all provisions: food, utensils, clothing and camping equipment. Bhageswaram is the ideal place to make these arrangements. The mules here are crossbreeds of donkeys and thoroughbred horses, and both mules and porters in this area have ample experience in climbing the steep hills with packs on their backs. The average weight taken by a mule is about 125 pounds or 57 kilograms; porters take half that much, or 60-65 pounds which is almost 30 kilograms.

8 June, Morning. We left Bhagaswaram and traveled the 14 miles to Kapcot by bus. The drivers had already left on foot with their

Top: The highway ahead.
Below: The pilgrim Swamis seated under a bodhi tree at Kapcot.

mules. The roadway on this stretch was being constructed that year and had yet to be macadamized, but the surface was dry and firm and we were able to ride on it with ease. Kapcot is 3,750 feet above sea level–a few hundred feet higher than our previous stop. We bathed in the river before lunch, and spent the rest of the day in the public works department rest house. Here our travel by vehicle came to an end. Our minds were looking forward to a pleasant journey on foot, which would enable us to enjoy the unsurpassed beauty of the hills at a much closer range. At the same time, the idea of climbing to the summit of a hill only to go down the other side, cross a valley and climb again was somewhat dampening to our enthusiasm. The only way to put our minds at ease was to clear them of all such thoughts, and remember instead our goal of the sight of Mount Kailash. We made a firm resolve that nothing would deter us from that goal.

"It is Time We Started"

9 June. We were bubbling with joy on this Monday morning. Before dawn–around five o'clock–preparations for our first day of walking had already begun. The drivers of the mules divided the baggage among their animals. The guide announced, "It is time we started," and with this, we took the very first steps of the long ascent.

The river Sarayu rushed down east, parallel to our route. A gentle wind, cooled by the river, distracted our minds. Green pastures, dotted with small flowers, spread out on either bank of the river like a Kashmir carpet. Our route continued for three and a half miles and then turned abruptly. We left the Sarayu behind, only to follow the bank of another river. There was a path leading to the Pindari glaciers from this point, but we passed it by in favor of the route to Milam. After a while we stopped for breakfast and a short rest. Lady Thackeray's delicacies served as our meal, together with some tea from a nearby kiosk. When we resumed our walk we found ourselves to be greatly refreshed.

A Very Narrow River

Around 1:30 in the afternoon we saw the outskirts of the village Siyamathara. We had covered eleven and a half miles since leaving Kapcot. The climb, although gradual at first, had suddenly become very steep. We soon learned that this kind of sudden change was to be expected. From a starting altitude of 3,750 feet, we had now reached 7,000 feet; 3,000 feet of the ascent had been covered over the last three and a half miles. This was our first experience of a climb that steep; there would be many more such climbs to come.

Siyamathara is a small, sparsely-populated village. We found accommodations for the night in the government rest house there. Our feet–imprisoned in heavy boots all day–found great solace in being released from their confinement. We longed for a bath to cool and refresh them. This place, like most of the stops along the way, has a river, but no one can bathe in its waters. Not because of the current, but because it is only an inch wide! We placed a small pan in the water where the river fell down over high rocks and held it there for some minutes. Eventually the pan was filled; we each soaked a cloth in it and used the wet cloths to wipe our bodies. Our bath accomplished, we had our evening meal and settled in for the night.

10 June. Our departure scheduled for this morning was delayed. The drivers of the mules also had to collect food and clothing for themselves before departing into the hills.

Chapter 6
Has This a Name?

We climbed to the top of the Siyamathara hill. The slope was very steep, but it did not take long to climb. And what a view it gave us! Our hearts leapt at the sight of Nanda Devi and the three peaks of Trisuli. We were very grateful to Siyamathara; although small in stature, it had nonetheless elevated us to a level where we could have this expanded view. A holy renunciate was living on the hilltop with a disciple. We stopped to pay him our respects and were soon joined by other pilgrims. The whole group chanted *bhajans,* and the holy atmosphere resounded with the names of God. The spiritual wisdom of this great sage elevated our consciousness, and we were completely immersed in discussion with him for a long time. Before departing, we asked him his name. His answer was, "Has this a name?"

"Who Am I?"

If we ask, "Who are you?" to those who have not yet delved into the spiritual side of life, we will get a variety of responses. "I am an American, I am an Indian, I am a businessman, a student, a doctor, rich, poor, male, female. . ." and on and on. All of these responses are different, and yet they all have the same beginning: "I am." Although the ending varies with one's country, career or other form of "I"-dentity, there is no difference whatsoever in the meaning of the "I"–the soul–of the first part. Before the "I" was identified with the different adjectives, it was simply "I." The "I" stood free, as soul consciousness. That soul is pure, unaffected by any conditions imposed upon it; it is bliss itself, always contented and at peace. One who has realized that pure soul cannot be bound by the limitations of name and country; he knows the limitless bliss of the Self.

The great soul on the hilltop did not limit himself with a name; we simply referred to him as Sri Maharaj–or revered king–in recognition

The author had to cross the Ram Ganga by walking on a single log seen in the center. Halfway across, the log would sway under his weight; if he stepped in time with it, he would reach the other bank . If not, he would drop into the rapids far below and reach Kailash quickly–in spirit.

of his spiritual greatness, which after all is the true wealth and nobility of human birth. After receiving the sage's blessings, we returned to the rest house. The next morning we descended along the path leading from Siyamathara to Quintee. The journey was pleasant enough over the gradual slope of the first five miles, but the following two miles posed great difficulty and took us down 3,000 more feet.

Bridge of Life

The famous Ram Ganga River is five miles from Quintee. It flows at a height of 4,000 feet with the combined force of waters rushing together from many sources in the hills. As it continues on its course, it freely gifts the lands it crosses with the wealth of its water. These mountain rivers remind one of Robin Hood, who stole from the rich to give to the hungry poor.

We became aware of the speed of Ram Ganga about half a mile from its bank. It is only 30 feet across and not very deep, yet extremely dangerous to cross. It rolls away even huge boulders with tremendous force. Any man attempting to wade across is certain to be swept away to the bosom of the ocean.

At the time of our trip, a modern bridge was being constructed across the river to take the place of the previous mode of crossing, which had been a bridge of ropes. Unfortunately, the old bridge had been removed, while the new bridge was not yet completed. As we stopped to figure out how we were to get across, we spotted a man just approaching the opposite bank. He came up to the edge and started walking across a very narrow log that had been placed across the river, high above the water. When he had successfully reached the other side, our porters set off across the log with the baggage on their shoulders. Then they returned to carry the mule packs, while the animals swam the swift waters below.

When my turn came to cross the narrow bridge, I cautiously stepped forward. By the time I reached the center of the river, my mind was firmly fixed on God and God alone. This was only partly out of devotion, however; it was mostly out of fear for my life. As one reached the middle of the crossing, his weight would cause the log to bow, and it would spring up and down under each step. If one did not shift his weight in rhythm with it, he would soon find himself swimming the rapids. The awareness of this ever-present possibility helped me to keep my undivided attention on each step.

Life is also a bridge. It springs high and low with pain and pleasure, fortune and misfortune. One must cross the river of birth and death amidst the swaying with a single-minded aim of God-realization. If our minds get distracted, we find ourselves tumbling down the steep precipices, groaning and gasping with the intense pain of the falls. The truths of life brought out in the course of this difficult pilgrimage were noble indeed!

On the opposite bank is an area where the course of the river is calmer. We refreshed ourselves by bathing there, and had some breakfast before proceeding.

Potholes in Our Beds

Quintee is located eight miles from Siyamathara at an elevation of 4,000 feet. A school there provided us with shelter for the night, and for the first time in our journey, Divan Singh began cooking. However, he only began. The very next moment, Swami Premanandaji insisted on taking over, and would not stop until each of us had been served. Such is his affectionate nature. How appropriate that he was given the name Premananda, which means the "bliss of divine love." After dinner we wanted to retire for the night and looked for an even space in which to spread out our bedding, but that was scarcely possible. The floor of the school was the image of the Himalayan range: full of potholes and rocky surfaces. Still, we were once again reminded of God's mercy. Although one of the porters had taken ill and would have to be replaced the next day, this man had become ill in a place where there was human habitation. It could just as well have happened out on the icy peaks. With that reassuring thought, we slept.

Gasping for Breath

12-19 June. Eight days of travel from the 4,000 foot high Quintee would take us to Milam at 12,500 feet. The distance between these two places is 56 miles. This part of the climb is especially noteworthy because of the varied and challenging terrain. Just two miles from Quintee was a wide plain, followed by five steep miles leading to a height of 9,000 feet–an incline of 1,000 feet per mile. We passed

Girham and came to the summit of the hill known as Kalamuni. When you are gasping for breath long before reaching the summit, you begin to understand that climbing Kailash really is a life-or-death venture. The legs plead with you, "Do you really have to climb all the way to the top of Mount Kailash? Is there nowhere else that you can see God? What is this foolishness? Why are you causing all this needless suffering?" Still, we were able to cajole our legs into cooperating, and soon reached the summit. There the cold was so severe that our bodies shook. The next two miles were a difficult descent. Since the sun was setting, it was impossible to think of proceeding any farther that night, and we looked around for shelter.

Pethuli Cave: A Rare Opportunity

We found a cave in the immediate vicinity and prepared to spend the night in this natural shelter provided by God. We ate, covered the rough, stony ground with leaves and shrubs, and spread out our sleeping bags. The insects and worms who were sharing their home with us moved about freely under our bed of greenery while we slept. I was soon awakened by the intense cold, and remained awake the rest of the night. The sounds of the jungle interrupted the crisp stillness at measured intervals. I will never forget this cave that offered me the rare opportunity to mingle with worms and insects, and to spend the night listening to the cries and whines of the wild night animals. This cave is known as Pethuli.

We Meet a Fox

The next morning we bade farewell to Pethuli and resumed our journey. We covered the next two miles–a steep and exhausting climb through thick jungle–at a slow, steady pace. At one point, a fox crossed our path. All of us were glad to see this animal, since it is commonly believed that a fox's crossing brings good luck. (The superstitious will say that you are lucky if a fox crosses your path; the non-superstitious will say that you are lucky if a fox crosses your path and does not tear you apart. Either way we were lucky.) A short distance from us was a group of shepherds, and we soon reached their tents. We were very grateful for the milk these men generously offered us. Whether or not it had to do with the fox, meeting the shepherds proved to be a pleasant stroke of luck.

We also met two brothers, named Ramlal and Laxmanalal. How kind-hearted they were! Upon hearing that we were pilgrims to Kailash, they became exuberant. Both brothers were staunch believers in God, and they gave us a *naya paise* each—a cent of an Indian rupee—with the request that the coins be offered at the feet of the Lord of Kailash. What faith they showed, not only in the Lord whose blessings they sought, but also in the pilgrims who they seemed to believe would successfully complete this difficult pilgrimage. In fulfillment of their wish, these coins were later dropped prayerfully into Lake Gowri.

A Mother of the Hill Tribe

As we proceeded along the path, we met a mother of the hill tribe carrying her baby in a basket strapped to her back. She wore a simple, tunic-like garment that hung from her shoulders to her ankles. A long cloth was wrapped around her waist. She also wore silver bangles and beads, and a nose-ring of about five inches in diameter. How constant was the mother's mindfulness of her beloved child as she patiently posed for a photograph. We happily accepted the *jaggery*, a kind of raw sugar, that she offered to us for having taken her picture. Her dark eyes shone with gratitude as we parted. It was now evening, and we had covered a total of nine miles since morning. We spent the night at the public works department rest house in Rethi.

Top: Swami Premanandaji cooking in front of Pethuli Cave. How can I express the greatness of his heart?
Below: A mother of the hill tribe, wearing a five-inch nose ring, seen posing for the camera. Her baby is sleeping on her back.

Even the goats are pilgrims going up to Kailash, but for a different purpose: carrying things.

Chapter 7
Rethi

Rethi–also known as Munsari–lies at a height of 5,000 feet. We were spellbound by the view of the snowy hills that we had from this point. During the winter, another 40 or 50 miles farther down the hillside would be covered with snow. The villagers living up there would close up their houses in the hills and come down here to spend the winter. Many of the small dwellings seen here are the winter homes of the hill people.

Rethi frequently faces a water shortage. It lies high above the valley where the Gowri Ganga flows, and cannot make use of the water from the river. In the sunny months the drought can be quite severe.

The tents we would be needing farther up in the hills were made to order at Rethi. A trader named Jagath Singh was of immense help in arranging for the tents. We got two. The one for sleeping, which could comfortably accommodate five people, was twelve feet by nine feet, and cost 80 rupees (about US $16 at the time). The second, smaller tent was to be used for cooking. These tents added considerably to the weight of the baggage, and another mule had to be hired.

Honey from the Hills

16 June. The path out of Rethi followed the banks of the Gowri Ganga. This river originates in the Milam glacier, and its steep course is rapid and rough. The Baldi Ganga comes from a higher elevation, flowing over a course of six miles before merging with Gowri Ganga. The point of entry is a spectacular sight. Gowri Ganga continues winding its way down the mountain–undaunted by thick forests, deep valleys and steep rock falls–and flows on out of sight. We saw a honeycomb amidst the steep, high rocks, and were amazed that anyone could take honey from it. But they do.

The men of the hill tribe collect this honey once a year. They smear their bodies with a paste to prevent the bees from stinging and climb the rocky paths. When they reach the top of the hill, they tie one end of a rope ladder to a tree and lower the other end along the rocks. Holding the rope ladder firmly, they climb down the rocks to reach the honeycomb. Most people would shudder at the mere thought, but the men who risk their lives in this way do extract the sweetest honey.

Action and Reaction

By noon we reached Rupshibagar, also called Sundara Medu or the "Mount of Beauty." It is eleven miles from Rethi. The pilgrim must be cautious while walking in these parts, since there is a species of plant growing wild along the path that produces a very irritating skin rash. These plants–similar to the *kanchuran* shrub found in South India–grow all along the northern borders of India; one must be very careful not to let them touch any part of the body. At Sundara Medu we pitched our tents for the first time.

The path from Sundara Medu to Milam follows the banks of the river. At one point on the opposite bank a warm spring bubbles continuously. The sulfur from the waters of the spring had dried on the rocks and reflected various colors under the bright rays of the sun.

We passed a herd of goats carrying small packs on their backs. Later we were to come across this species quite often. Twin bags of provisions hung across each animal's back and down its sides. The weight on one of the goats was not properly balanced, and the animal was staggering. I put my staff under my arm so that I could adjust the weight on its back. At that moment, I heard a murmur and looked over my shoulder. Swami Bagawathanandaji, who had been following me, was rubbing his thigh. I realized that my spiked staff had pricked Swamiji's leg. I immediately apologized, but the incident reminded me of another that had happened just a few hours earlier. Swami Bagawathanandaji had accidently injured one of my feet with his staff. Now he had been accidentally injured by my staff. A great truth became apparent from this incident: one must reap the results of an action, whether or not that action is intentional.

Top: Close-up of a Tibetan "freight train"–a herd of goats carrying baggage. The brawny leader in the foreground must be their locomotive.
Below: Traders' merchandise from last year sits on the rocks at Bagutyar, waiting to be picked up this year. No guard, no theft.

No Watcher and No Theft

We proceeded further and came to Bagutyar, the "place of many caves." Here we found some valuables and grains, which had been piled on rocks in an open space and covered with a tarpaulin to protect them from the sun and rain. I asked to whom they belonged and why they had been left there, and learned that they belonged to the traders who traveled farther up into the hills. The traders traveling to Tibet leave a part of their merchandise here in bundles and continue on to Milam. Two or three weeks later they return to collect their belongings. There simply are not enough mules to transport the entire consignment in one lot, so they leave some of it here in the care of God. No one is engaged to watch the goods, and no thief touches them. The people of the hill tribes are labeled as uncivilized—and yet how cultured and God-fearing they are! I wondered if they were actually a part of our modern world, where each one snatches from the next whatever he can to enrich himself and satisfy an ever-increasing number of personal "needs." It seems that this uncivilized life is far better than that of the cities.

Nehar and Cold

We climbed to an altitude of 8,000 feet and reached Nehar. Nehar is a familiar name, and many people think that it is a city. Actually, it is a wide, open valley. At this point the ground was covered with thick snow, and we were getting ahead of the mules and porters who were unable to continue at their previous pace. For the first time in our journey, we saw the rivers iced over in places. The clear blue sky suddenly became dark. There was a gust of wind, and rain came down in torrents. We looked around the rocks for some kind of niche or overhang that could provide us with shelter. Finding none, we made a temporary tent with canvas; this at least kept us from getting soaked. After some time, the porters arrived with the baggage. We pitched our tent and huddled inside, which helped to somewhat ease the cold as well.

On the climb up from Nehar, large areas of frozen snow were seen more frequently. Frozen patches on the rivers often served as bridges for crossing, even though it was certain that if the bridge were to crack, the pilgrim would end up in the bosom of the river, never to be retrieved. The first five miles from Nehar was a gradual climb, but the next three were extremely steep. Still, we were able to reach Martholi at 12,222 feet that same day.

Martholi is severely cold in the month of June. For the first time on our journey, we found that we needed to get out all of the woolens we had brought. This substantially reduced the load on the mules. That evening we visited the nearby Bagawathi temple. That night was spent in the village.

Nanda Devi Poses

The next morning we started down a steep decline. A mile farther we came to an equally steep incline leading to a wide, flat area. This flat stretch gave us some relief before we had to climb again. We had crossed the Gowri Ganga and continued five miles along the opposite bank, when the thrilling sight of Nanda Devi and Trisuli came into view. Before I could even get out my camera, they had disappeared behind the clouds. I patiently waited for another glimpse. Nanda Devi took pity on me after a while, and emerged from her cover to present a reasonably-clear picture. I felt fortunate to be able to photograph her and worship her profusely before rejoining the group. Within a short time, we were able to spot some tents in the distance; this would be the village of Milam.

We eagerly looked forward to resting there. When we arrived, the porters and drivers of the mules who had transported our baggage thus far asked to be paid off. We settled their accounts and thanked them profusely. They departed, wishing us a pleasant journey.

Top: Nanda Devi poses in her tall crown of frozen snow.
Below: A short rest under our temporary tent.

Chapter 8
Milam: An Unscheduled Stop

Milam, the last village on the path to the Tibetan border, lies at an altitude of 12,500 feet. There are about 350 houses in this hamlet. During the winter months, the entire village is buried in snow and the cold is so severe that neither plants nor animals can survive. The residents here, as mentioned earlier, migrate down the hill to other villages. When spring sets in, they return the 50 miles or so to Milam, re-establishing the school, post office and courts on their return. Every aspect of life is temporary in this place, and when it begins to snow again, the inhabitants rush back down to the lower elevations.

There are times when even the villages to which they have escaped get enveloped by the snow. Then they move another 20 or 30 miles down the mountainside. Migrating down the slopes during the winter and returning to the peaks in the spring is an annual routine of the hill tribes. Each family has houses at two or three different stations. The scenery around Milam is breathtaking, and the atmosphere is filled with holy vibrations, but this is not the only reason for the return to the hills each spring. These people simply cannot bear the heat at the lower altitudes.

Most of the villagers of Milam are traders. There are a few farmers here, but their small, cultivated plots are rare sights. No other occupation is evident. Although both men and women migrate to Milam in the spring, it is the women who spend the full season there. The men frequently spend the warm months traveling to the Tibetan villages for trading. On the day we reached Milam, Divan Singh started looking around for firewood, but it was like looking for water in the desert. Nothing grows in this open village. Because there is no grazing land, animals are also rare and, consequently, so are milk and *ghee*.

Gowri Ganga is a long distance away, and the task of transporting her water to Milam could make a man cry. All provisions are very dear.

Top: School building at Milam built by a Christian missionary in 1937. However, he found that he couldn't get any converts and left the place. Now, the village runs the school.
Below: A gathering of the Indian border police for the *Guru Poornima* celebration at Milam.

Top: A broken-down part of the Milam
Glacier, which has formed a pond of
icy water.
Below: Crossing an icy "bridge."

Everything has to be brought in across difficult terrain from areas far below, and the prices rise with the altitude. A can of kerosene oil, costing only three or four rupees in one of the towns below, costs 20 to 30 rupees in Milam.

Nevertheless, the villagers are friendly and affectionate. It seemed as if Mother Nature meant for us to experience the warm hearts of these people, because the path leading beyond Milam was blocked by ice and snow, and we were forced to spend 15 days there.

The School at Milam

Classes had not yet resumed that spring, and we were able to make the school building our home for the duration of our stay. In fact, the classes were just starting again as we were leaving. It seemed that each event along our journey—even the unexpected ones—were part of a perfectly-timed plan. Though school was not officially in session, the children of the village loved to gather in the building. They romped and played there throughout the days of our stay, and their sweet prattle swept us away into a world of simple joy.

The school building, constructed in 1937, is a monument to the service of a Christian missionary who attempted to spread his religion in the thinly-populated village by building a school for the children. The inhabitants, however, were already staunch Hindus and could not be converted. After some time, the missionary gave up and left the area. Though the villagers did not adopt his faith, they nevertheless remember him fondly for having given their children a school.

We realized after a while that the tents we had sighted from the outskirts of Milam were actually the camps of the Indian border police. These men were very friendly, and proved to be good company during our stay in this outpost.

Milam Glacier

22 June. We left this morning to see the famous Milam glacier. Mules and porters were specially engaged for the two-day trip. We started out with a gradual climb over the first mile, but the following few miles were a tortuous steep ascent. The entire

distance was covered with icy, granular snow. The air was so thin that we were all soon exhausted from lack of oxygen. We had to halt at every step to catch our breath, as we went higher and higher, until we were scarcely able to breathe at all. This made us acutely aware that the simple involuntary act of breathing in and out, which man normally takes for granted, can also cease involuntarily at any moment. This was our first experience of such a formidable climb, and we were only able to cover four miles between early morning and noon.

Lake Sandilya: A Blissful Night

We had climbed to a height of approximately 13,000 feet when we pitched our camp near Lake Sandilya, named after the great saint who had performed penance there. The divine vibrations that filled the air soon filled us as well. We rejoiced in a bath in the lake, followed by a satisfying lunch, and were all surprised to find ourselves recovering so quickly from the extreme fatigue of the climb. That afternoon was spent enjoying the surroundings and discussing our experiences. After a light evening meal, we retired for the night.

As it turned out, I only spent a few minutes in bed. Some unknown force kindled me from within. I suddenly became aware of a pleasant feeling, both within and without, that words cannot express. Reluctant to stay in the tent, I put on a woolen shawl and left for the shore of the lake. There I sat in meditation. What calmness! What peace! What joy! The Lord blessed me with the wonderful bliss of sleep with consciousness. I lost myself in that bliss.

I did not realize how much time had passed until the first brilliant rays of morning sunlight reflected off the glacier, piercing my eyelids. The inner light gradually sank back into the heart, while the eyes became alive to the outer light. The mind, still immersed in the joy of the inner light, made the eyes gently close their lids once more. This gentle tug back and forth between the inner light and the outer light went on for some time. The ears, which had only heard the inner sound of *OM* in that blissful state, now became aware of the heavy movements of men and mules. Little by little I became conscious of the outer world. But even while moving about in the world, that bliss within—once experienced—is never to be forgotten.

Lake Surya Kundam

23 June. In the morning we left the mules and the camp on the bank of Lake Sandilya and proceeded towards Lake Surya Kundam. Sun, rain, cold and snow greeted us in turn along the way. These changes seemed to emphasize the cycle of pain and pleasure that follow in turn in one's life. The entire walk was on frozen snow. Even though the mind was willing, the body was weak with fatigue, and I had to give up the climb when I was only a short distance from the lake on the glacier.

Along the climb we saw broad crevasses in the frozen snow. It was so still that we could hear the murmur of water running deep below. Likewise, can we not hear the divine murmur arising from that spring of love deep within the heart, if only the external senses stop their noise? A stone fell into a crevasse, and we listened to it race downward; it was a long time before we heard it splash into the water far below. The thought of falling into one of those crevasses made one shudder. Farther down the slope, this water surfaced as Gowri Ganga.

While the rest of the group ascended the glacier, I stayed behind and enjoyed the scenery with Swami Bagawathananda, who was also overcome with fatigue. Clear water ran like small canals on top of the glaciers. Layers of clear, fresh snow covered the canals like sheets of glass. We finally departed from here with great reluctance and took our time going back to the camp on the shore of Lake Sandilya.

Some Useful Plants

A beautiful plant called *thanthoori* grows in abundance around Lake Sandilya. It has broad dark green leaves and red stalk-like flowers. The stem of the leaves and plant are edible. They have a sweet-and-sour taste similar to that of partly matured grapes or the *nelli* (gooseberry) fruit of South India and Sri Lanka. The juice of the roots is used as saffron color dye for clothes.

Another plant commonly found here is *thuloo*. The juice of the roots is very much like tincture of iodine, and the inhabitants of the area use it to treat injuries.

We retired for the night after dinner. I spent another night of conscious sleep as I had the night before. On the morning of the

24th, we went back to Milam and stayed there through the 2nd of July. This unscheduled stop used up a good portion of the provisions we had brought along for the entire trip, and we now had to restock. It was no use fainting on hearing the prices. We procured whatever further provisions were needed and engaged new porters and mules to replace those we had paid off upon arrival.

Bathing happily in Sandilya Lake, named after the great saint who performed penance there.

Top: Brother and sister carrying water. To get a drop from the river a mile below, you have to shed a drop from your eye. Yet see how happy they are.

Below: A nice feast is served to the villagers after the *Guru Poornima* festivities.

Chapter 9
The Hospitality of the Hill Tribes

24 June, Evening. We met two men who had just come to Milam from Tibet. They were the first men to cross the snow-covered passes that year, and their arrival would serve as a signal to others that the path between the two places was now clear. The snow that had detained the pilgrims on their way to the holy abode of the Lord of Kailash was in retreat, deformed and demoralized by the advancing rays of the sun. The ways of nature are a never-ending wonder.

A Tale from the Past

In ancient days, permission to enter Tibet across the snow-covered passes was delivered by a messenger of the state. When the snow had melted, the messenger would break a stone in two and leave one piece in the custody of the Tibetan officials. He would take the other piece to the Indian-border post at Milam and give it to the traders. Any man seeking to enter Tibet would be asked to produce the stone. If their piece matched the one held by the state, they would be welcomed as honest traders. If the stone they presented did not fit, they were assumed to be enemies or robbers trying to deceive the officials and were put to death. Of course, this is a story of long ago.

Guru Poornima: A Grand Celebration

30 June. There was a loud babble of voices and great excitement as we all prepared to celebrate *Guru Poornima* on the following day. This is the auspicious full moon day set aside each year for honoring the spiritual teacher, who is the embodiment of the Lord's grace, and we were all determined to celebrate in a fitting manner. The day's activities were to include worship, offerings, programs and a huge feast. Food would be served to over 300 people, and the butter, ghee, flour and

other provisions took up a large part of the school hall. Divan Singh was not the least bit unnerved about the cooking, however, since many of the mothers—and children as well—had eagerly volunteered to help.

1 July. The great holy day of *Guru Poornima*. We rose early in the morning and went to the Gowri Ganga to bathe. Our morning prayers and worship were performed at the river's edge as the sun was rising. There were great feelings of love, as well as devotion, in our worship, and it left us all in high spirits. We applied holy ash to one another's forehead and exchanged blessings before returning to the village to prepare for the grand feast. Some of the children helped us carry water from a distant spring. Others made hundreds of *puris*, which the mothers fried. Divan Singh contributed his share to the preparations, and more. Topping everyone else, of course, was Swami Premanandaji, who prepared the *halva*, sweet rice, *subji*, curry, *dhal* and vegetables with his customary zeal.

At nine in the morning, the people from Milam and the surrounding area gathered. They were all ready and eager to watch a special program to be presented by the children. What a joy that was for everyone: for the children, so proud to be giving the program, for the parents, so proud of their children, and for the pilgrims, who felt privileged to be witnessing this special event. The air was charged as the audience waited attentively for the program to begin. First, a welcome address was read on behalf of the children. This was a verbal expression of all the love and affection they had been showering on everyone over the last few days. Then the little girls came into the stage area, holding hands. They entertained us with a folk dance known as *kummi*, performing the steps gracefully and clapping their hands in rhythm, with smiles beaming on their bright faces.

"Sinnu Munnu"

The boys performed next. They started with a song called "Sinnu Munnu." One bright boy, attractively dressed, stood in the center of the group to serve as the leader. He started singing in a clear, sweet voice, and the others joined him.

Leader: How did Sinnu Munnu clap the tune?

Boys: Sinnu Munnu clapped the tune Thith Thorn, and clapped the tune again.

Leader: How did Sinnu Munnu beat the drum?

Boys: Sinnu Munnu clapping the tune Thith Thom, Thith Thorn beat the drum Dum Dum, Dum Dum, Dum Dum.

Leader: How did Sinnu Munnu play the flute?

Boys: Sinnu Munnu clapping the tune Thith Thom, Thith Thorn beating the drum.

Dum Dum, Dum Dum, Dum Dum played the flute Pip-pi Pip-pi Pip-pi.

Chorus: Sinnu Munnu clapping the tune Thith Thom, Thith Thom beating the drum

Dum Dum, Dum Dum, Dum Dum played the flute Pip-pi Pip-pi.

The boys were skillfully accompanied on a musical instrument, which even further delighted the audience. Everyone was very much impressed with the quality of the performance.

A few more such items were presented before the program came to an end. The great Tamil saint Thiruvalluvar says, "When there is no food for the ear, a little should be offered for the stomach." The program now being over, about 200 children were served the meal they had helped to prepare. At noon, some renunciates and the devotees from the village were also served. At six in the evening, there were more programs. The border police, led by their chief, Mr. Joshi, were asked to give a number of talks, as were Swami Premanandaji and myself. Then the villagers, knowing we were to leave the following day, took us in procession to the village. We were received there with great kindness and reverence, and the celebrations continued with *bhajans* and speeches until late at night.

A Storm Amidst the Calm

2 July, Morning. We were graciously hosted for a farewell breakfast by Mr. Lakshman Singh, one of the residents of Milam. The meal he so generously served to all of the pilgrims was a hearty send-off, satisfying to both body and spirit.

After breakfast, like a storm amidst the calm, the newly-hired mule drivers started an uproar. One shouted that his animal could not possibly carry such a heavy load, another that his mule had never before had so much weight on its back. Each and every driver was complaining loudly that the load on his animal was excessive. We found out that some cunning drivers had left early with their mules, taking only the light bedding as their share of the load. The others now claimed that the rest of the baggage was too heavy, and refused to carry it. We also found out, however, that the loads were no more than the animals normally took, and that it was a habit of the drivers to create discord whether the load was heavy or not. We had an awful time trying to redistribute the baggage among the seven mules to the satisfaction of the drivers. Their non-cooperation was a terrible nuisance. Fortunately, Mr. Joshi had come to see us off, and the dispute was finally settled through his intervention. We were now able to start the day's journey.

The villagers also came to see us off, and we were touched by the kind and sincere sentiments they expressed. Of course, the children were there, too, chanting the names of God with angelic voices. The mule drivers, fighting in the midst of all this love and affection, proved once again the truth of the saying, "Pain and pleasure are but two sides of the same coin."

May Such Kindness Live Forever

The seven mules, now loaded with baggage, started off down the path. The four we had hired for riding followed along behind us. All of the residents of Milam—men, women and children of all ages, from very young to very old—gathered in a grand parade led by musicians. The long procession, a visible demonstration of the deep and sincere love of these simple people, came up to the very outskirts of the village. Each one of them individually wished us farewell. Some of them even followed us to the top of the hill, where they stood watching us descend until we had disappeared from sight. May the hospitality and kindness of the people of Milam be full and alive forever.

Top: The school at Milam in session again.
Below: A royal send-off: the entire village of Milam accompanying the pilgrims
to the edge of town.

Top: Undathura Pass: ice and snow at 18,500 feet.
Below: The plight of the mules: all four legs buried in snow.

Chapter 10

More Demands on Behalf of the Mules

2 July, Evening. We arrived at Mala Shilong, five miles from Milam, and camped there for the night. That same evening a small group of pilgrims from Almora set up camp nearby, and we all agreed to travel together from that point on.

3 July. The night passed away and the morning sun rose. While preparing to leave, we made sure that the baggage was distributed equally among the mules. Nevertheless, the drivers started a dispute, once again delaying our departure. This time they demanded that we pay their wages in full in advance. We did not think it reasonable to be expected to pay for a job before it was performed. They argued that they stood the risk of being robbed on the return trip and, therefore, should be paid in full beforehand. They would not give up their mulishness easily, and we finally had to agree to advance them at least a part of the sum. It was nine o'clock before we were able to start the day's climb.

Undathura Pass: Ice and Cold at 18,500 Feet

Undathura Pass is eight miles from Mala Shilong at an elevation of 18,500 feet. The first five miles of the climb is a gradual rise, the final stretch fearfully steep. The path was covered at intervals with frozen snow, and the mules suffered severely. It was heart-rending to see them struggling to pull their legs out of the snow with each step. At times, all four legs would get stuck; we would then have to shove some heavy sticks under their bellies and lift them out of their entrapment. At a number of spots, the mules toppled over, scattering the baggage. It did not take long for the provisions to get soaked. Each time, we would have to collect the wet baggage, and secure it on their backs again. At other places, the deep granular snow was covered by a layer of soft, fresh powder. The feet of the mules were often cut by the sharp, icy edges of crevasses lying hidden below.

Our legs also broke through the frozen snow at times. If one foot sank, the other had to be firmly braced while the leg was extricated and moved ahead. If the pilgrim got excited or alarmed and did not act swiftly and surely, the leg would sink deeper and deeper. If he hastily put the free leg forward, both feet would sink and he would need assistance to get out. Fellow pilgrims would come quickly, knowing that those feet might soon be frozen in place. Furthermore, both men and mules faced the danger of slipping on the steep path, and tumbling down the slope nonstop, until they found themselves in the middle of one of the bitter-cold streams of melted snow.

We were all exhausted when we reached the peak of Undathura Pass at five in the evening. Although we longed to set up camp and rest, we found the pass to be unbearable. This was a very high spot, and the wind gleefully joined the cold in its chilling task of discomfiting the pilgrims. We had no choice but to climb down the slope. It was a treacherous descent, and the slipperiness of the snow melting in the afternoon sun added to the already-existing dangers. We took every step with great caution and the firm support of our staffs; not doing so would have meant either rising from frequent falls or falling never to rise again. The grace of God brought us safely to the bottom of the slope; there we looked back to find that the mules and drivers had not been following us. The descent, formidable for men, had proved impossible for the mules. It was eight at night, and we shivered from the piercing cold. Our tents, food and bedding were with the mules at the top of the slope we had just descended.

We now faced the Gangapaani Valley, a frozen plain about half a mile across. As we entered the valley we were amazed to see a tent in the distance. Assuming this to be the camp of another group of pilgrims like ourselves, we hurried in that direction. When we reached the tent we were surprised to find instead that it was a tea kiosk set up only the night before by Pratap Singh and his son Gushall Singh.

Life in the Tent

It was a small tent, eight feet by eight feet at the base, and Pratap Singh made room for us inside by stepping out into the snow. All of us squeezed in and drank the tea he had made. It is not possible to put into words the sacrifice that Pratap Singh made by offering us his tent. There was a slight drizzle of rain outside, and the wind was merciless. In a short time, we pleaded that he also come inside. Fifteen of us huddled together in that miniature tent. Pratap Singh's saddle and provisions took up a quarter of the space, and there was also a fire. Still, to us this was a palace. There were no flaps to cover the open end of the tent, and we suffered from pangs of cold in spite of the fire. Some of us were soon afflicted with headaches from lack of oxygen as well. The pills we had with us brought some relief. All of us were overcome by heavy fatigue, and our bodies demanded sleep. I looked around the tent. Lying down was impossible; there was barely enough room to sit! Heads rolled to one side or the other as the pilgrims dozed off in whatever position they found themselves. Some leaned against the baggage beside them. Others slept upright, as if seated in meditation. I was sitting on a boulder that served as a base for one edge of the tent. Pratap Singh's baggage and saddle had been used to fill the opening between the tent and the rock; nevertheless, the cold wind beat through, numbing my buttocks. I rested my head between my knees and immersed myself in thoughts of the Lord.

Thus we prepared to spend the night, in a tent pitched on frozen snow, in a valley surrounded by snow-covered mountains, at an elevation of 18,500 feet, with rain beating down incessantly. There was no ventilation, and the fire used to make the tea smoked continuously. Those inside woke often, and drank the salted tea each time they woke.

Top: Mules carry baggage; people pull them out of the snow.
Below: A mule sunk in the snow struggles to extricate itself; the Sherpas help.
It is not easy to measure the mules' sacrifice for us.

Chapter 11
The Plight of the Mules

The drivers had been slowly following us at a distance with the mules. When they reached the Undathura Pass, they hesitated to follow us down the steep slope, deciding instead to unload the animals and take them back to a spot that we had passed earlier for the night. Once they had been relieved of their load, the mules usually liked to roll on the ground, but here the rough stones and ice hurt so much that they immediately scrambled back to their feet. Having given up their rolling, they now looked around for pasture to graze.

Hunger cares little where one is, and the mules were in its clutches. The ground around them was covered with barren snow, but something on the back of one of their mates looked like grass. It was actually the animal's shaggy coat, but the mules were blinded by hunger, and each one began to chew the hair on the back of another. Within a few minutes all of the mules were biting and kicking in confusion. The drivers were horrified. They had seen this kind of thing before and knew that if the melee were allowed to continue, not a single mule would survive. This was almost a certainty. Leaving the baggage then and there in the care of God, they quickly led the mules back down the slope about two or three miles to a place where they had seen some grass. There they spent the night. Two of the drivers took pity on us and attempted the descent instead. One of them managed to get his mule to our camp, where he awaited the arrival of the other.

Ho! My Mule is Lost!

About ten o'clock, as we were dozing in Pratap Singh's tent, we suddenly heard someone wailing outside. We looked out to see the young Maan Singh running towards us shouting, "Ho, my mule is lost! What shall I do? What shall I do?" We knew that the animal would be in great danger, and immediately asked him for details. He told us that his mule had stumbled on the hillside and rolled on down out of sight. We were stunned. The animal could be anywhere on the snow-covered slope, or even in the valley itself. It had taken us hours to cover that distance in the daylight; finding a mule at this time of night seemed an impossible task. It was certainly a dangerous one. Still, two kind-hearted men went out–their path lit by flashlights and the stars–to attempt a rescue. A long search did bring them to the mule, but in spite of all their efforts they were not able to free the poor animal, whose legs were very deeply imbedded in the snow. They returned to camp in defeat, but explained that we need not fear for the life of the animal, since only its feet had been buried. They would make another attempt at rescue in the morning.

We brought Maan Singh into the tent and gave him some tea. While the others tried to console him, I mentally repeated the *Maha Mrityunjaya mantra*, a prayer for the welfare of all beings. Maan Singh gradually stopped his crying and began doing Ram *japa*. As he quietly repeated the name of God, the other inmates dozed off and the tent finally became silent once more. I was still awake around two o'clock when Divan Singh woke up and affectionately inquired if I had slept. He offered to make some tea, and I gratefully accepted.

The Worry is Over

Our conversation roused those who were only half asleep, and they decided to join us for tea. While waiting for Divan Singh to prepare it, we heard the distant neigh of a mule. We all assumed it to be that of Maan Singh, and were greatly relieved. When we had finished our tea, the others returned to their former state of half-sleep.

I was still wide awake, and spent the rest of the night waiting for the sun to come up. Rain fell the whole time. As the first rays of dawn appeared, Maan Singh quietly left in search of his mule. He returned about 45 minutes later with the news that the animal had reached Kailash ahead of us all. Ram *japa* was forgotten, and the youngster once again wailed loudly. Each of us–in his own way–tried to console the boy, but none of us succeeded. Our words might have consoled him if he had been worried about the departed soul of the mule, but as it turned out, his primary concern was the loss of its value. Once we discovered this, we offered to compensate him for the loss and, thus, were finally able to bring him back to his normal spirits.

As the sun rose over the horizon, the pilgrims came out into the daylight. The body of the unfortunate mule which had tumbled down the slope and faced its death in the merciless cold was only half a mile away. It was a pitiful sight. Within just a few more minutes, the carcass of the dead animal had become a feast for a number of giant vultures. Such is the way of the world. One's loss is another's gain; one's pleasure, another's pain.

An Original Means of Transport

The drivers who had gone back to the grazing area the night before climbed to the Undathura Pass again that morning, and again wavered over the descent. At first they refused to come down at all. Then they considered bringing the baggage down but leaving the mules behind. They finally decided to bring the mules down and leave the baggage. The animals struggled terribly on the descent. One mule stumbled and slid all the way down the slope, just as Maan Singh's had done the day before–but this one took its master along with it. Immediate rescue was possible this time, however, and both mule and driver were spared departure from this world. At times, the condition of the path is so treacherous that drivers will not even attempt to lead the mules down; instead, they tie the legs of the animals, wrap their bodies in thick woolen rugs and slide them down the slopes.

By late morning the mules had all arrived at the camp. In the afternoon a few men went back up and slid part of our baggage down the hill. The rest of it was left unattended at the Pass. Since our camping equipment and bedding had thus arrived, we put up our tents and prepared to spend another night in the Gangapaani Valley. These accommodations were luxurious compared to the tea kiosk of the night before, but when the sun went down, the cold commenced its reign and the pilgrims began to shiver again. The temperature, which was often as high as 28°C (83°F) during the day, usually dropped to 9°C (48°F) after sunset and 3° (38°F) by morning. There was nothing on the hilltops, other than our own tents, to break the course of the icy wind as it swept across the glaciers. I got into my sleeping bag, but the cold penetrated even that and my body was soon chilled. Nevertheless, it was warmer than the snow beneath it, which soon melted, soaking through the canvas under my bedding. A headache that had begun earlier in the evening increased in intensity as the night progressed, and I slept fitfully.

Facing Death

Shortly before midnight my body began to shake violently. My heartbeat slowed dramatically, and I could scarcely breathe. It seemed certain that this body was not going to reach Kailash. It is not possible to describe the feeling one gets when he sees the life departing from his own body, and knows that he is helpless to stop it. All I could do was pray: "Oh Lord! I have come all the way here to worship You in Your holy abode. Am I not fit to do so?" I struggled to sit up and fought for breath as I continued to pray. In a short while, my body began to sweat profusely. Little by little, the life that had almost departed from this frame seeped back in. Within another half hour, both respiration and heartbeat had stabilized. Relieved to some extent, I was able to get back into my sleeping bag. I spent the rest of the night thanking the Lord for His mercy.

5 July, Morning. The mule drivers brought down the rest of our baggage, one piece at a time. They applied themselves to this task in a half-hearted way, and night had set in by the time they finished. When the baggage was unpacked, several items were missing: the bedding of Ramdas, who had recently joined us; a woolen blanket belonging to Kunthan Singh; a teapot; the container of *ghee* and a few other things. The driver who had safely reached our camp the night before had brought the food provisions, and those too had been short. All of the drivers, when asked about this, pleaded total ignorance. There was no way of knowing if we had been robbed or if the drivers had simply felt free to help themselves to these goods. That night was more comfortable than the previous one, and I was able to sleep peacefully. Still, some unknown force woke me at two o'clock in the morning, and I sat in meditation until dawn.

A Stream Blocks the Path

6 July, Morning. We proceeded from Gangapaani at last. Some members of the group were already on their way by eight o'clock.

The rest of us waited for the mules to arrive; they had been taken to graze in a grassier spot, and it was eleven by the time they returned. We hired Pratap Singh's mule to replace the one lost by Maan Singh, and another one as well, bringing the total number of animals to twelve.

A three-hour walk over a distance of four miles took us through Dobithunga and on to Sumnath. Here we again came across one of the many streams that originated from snow melting in the hills. Those who had left camp early had crossed the stream when the snow was frozen. By the time we arrived, it had started to melt and the stream was in full spate. The drivers unloaded the animals on the bank, declaring that it was impossible to cross the stream at that time and we would have to wait until morning.

The group of pilgrims was now divided on opposite banks of the stream. Those on our side had the food, clothing and tents. A group of traders helped those on the opposite side with food and clothing, and we sent them bedding by a means of air transport that could not be hindered by the swollen stream. We simply threw some blankets and sleeping bags across the water. Life is not a passage of endless victory; neither is it one of total defeat.

The Fate of the *Brahmachari*

The pilgrims on our bank had dinner, chanted *bhajans* and retired for the night. The next morning we went to bathe in the river as usual. There we found a woolen shirt, a sheepskin, a saffron colored bag and a few other personal items on the bank. We recognized them at once as belonging to a *brahmachari* who had been traveling with us off and on. In fact, this young monk had spent the night of the third in Pratap Singh's tent with us. Had he accidently drowned while bathing, or was it a suicide? There was no way of knowing. May his soul rest in peace.

We left Sumnath that morning. The river was shallow again, and we were able to cross with ease. The eight miles taking us on to Kinguru Pass proved to be a test of tolerance for our feet. The terrain was also difficult on the four miles across the Pass, but the sight of high glacial cliffs, rushing rivers and hills in the shape of Buddhist *dagobas* eased our fatigue. We were able to reach Lipthal that same day.

Top: The Gangapaani tea kiosk that sheltered us from the freezing snow, and Pratap Singh, the benevolent owner who was willing to risk his own life in order to preserve ours.

Below: The baggage that was rolled down the hills the previous evening is being dragged back to the tent the following morning.

Chapter 12
We Reach Tibet

8 July. On this day our journey in Bharat (India) would come to an end. We were on our way to Palche Pass, which lies on the Indo-Tibetan border. Palche Pass is not far from Lipthal, but the path to it is a steep, continuous uphill climb. The mules were soon exhausted and gasping for breath. Their abdomens heaved as they forced the air in and out, and their labored breathing sounded like the rasping of a blacksmith's bellows. Even the mule that had carried me ahead of all the others the day before was now staggering. I bade my tired legs to relieve the poor animal and carry me again. One should remember that mule rides in the Himalayas are never lengthy. Of the fifteen miles that might be traveled in a day, ten to twelve will be covered on foot. Only the remaining few miles are traveled by riding, and even this is done in short stretches with long intervals of walking in between.

Piercing Cold and Gale-Force Winds

It took all of our strength to reach the peaks of Palche Pass. There the howling wind soon had us shivering again. I mentally found fault with the guide; a good guide should warn the pilgrims in advance about the ascents, descents and climatic changes that lay ahead. I told him regretfully that if I had known this was coming I could have brought something from my pack to protect myself from the piercing cold wind.

At the same time, I tried to remember that even if the guide falls short in his duty, he is still an instrument of God. A pilgrim should face all of the pains and trials of the journey with patience and forbearance. The thought that this, too, was part of the pilgrimage brought some mental relief, although physically we were all spent. One of the drivers told us some harrowing stories of the havoc sometimes caused by the gale-force winds here. Their velocity can be so great that unsuspecting goats grazing on the hillside are suddenly carried high into the sky. At times the winds even lift up human beings, taking their souls higher still, while casting their bodies back to the earth below. These stories were quite startling to hear as we trudged onward, struggling to brace ourselves against the driving wind. Fortunately, God did not see fit to uplift our spirits with these gales. We reached Tibet safely, and shortly thereafter came to Jangu, situated on the banks of the River Latha. There we spent the night.

The Rooftop of the World

Now that we are in Tibet, we should know a little bit about this part of the world. The Tibetan tableland–acclaimed as the "rooftop of the world"–is the highest elevation of human habitation, with an average range of 12,000 to 16,000 feet. There are many glaciers to be found in the heights of this region. The land covers an area of about 814,000 square miles, with a population of 400,000 scattered across it. Lhasa, the capital, lies at 12,890 feet, but the Tibetan people live at elevations as high as 17,000 feet.

Traveling in Tibet is like traveling on the limitless ocean: one can go many miles without meeting a fellow being. Buddhist monasteries dot the countryside here and there, but the distances between them are great. Villages are even farther apart. The land itself, however, is mostly open plain, and it is possible to walk long distances without getting tired. Supplies are carried by goats and by yak, a species of domesticated oxen with a thick coat of long matted hair that hangs down almost to the ground. There are no facilities here for pilgrims. The only roads are footpaths, and the only vehicles are the legs of the men and animals who tread them. Traveling this vast expanse of uninhabited land without a guide would be a formidable task.

Sightseeing

The path through the plains offers great variety. In some places, the surface is covered with multicolored sand that glitters in the sunlight. In other spots, the same path is covered with pebbles and stones; these are so sharp that they actually hurt your feet–even through heavy boots–and hinder progress. Other parts of the path are edged with small mounds of stones which Mother Nature has frosted with pure white snow. Even though there is no vegetation here, she has provided the landscape with plenty of color, constructing fascinating mosaics all along the horizon with stones in various shades of coral and emerald.

There are no tall trees in Tibet; the forests here are full of a kind of thorny shrub that stands about 18 inches high and is popularly called *dama*. These shrubs grow only in the warm months; in winter, they disappear. Tibet, being a tableland at a very great height, does not have heavy rainfalls. Instead, her water comes from showers of snow and hail.

Goats and cattle are plentiful in Tibet. The black goats can be seen wandering along the slopes of the hills in long lines. Rabbits abound around the thick patches of *dama*, but they jump into the shrubs to hide at the slightest sound. In some places, wild horses can be seen roaming freely.

The Fur of the Yak

The yak—*kavari* ox or *savari* ox in Tamil—is a very useful animal that is greatly appreciated by the Tibetans. The meadows are full of these animals, whose distinctive black and white coats can be easily spotted from a distance. The coarse white hair from their tails is made into fly whisks, commonly used to fan the deities in temples as well as the royalty in palaces. The black hair of the yak is used by Tibetan women to lengthen and beautify their own hair. The Tibetans also raise donkeys and an animal known as *jappu*. The *jappu* is a crossbreed of the Indian cow and the Tibetan yak. Birds are rare here, but one that looks very much like the crow—black with yellow beak and legs—is sometimes seen.

The Tibetan People We Saw

The Tibetans have strong, well-formed physical features. They also have strong constitutions, with a great capacity for hard work and a great tolerance for extreme cold. In spite of their staunch beliefs in the olden ways, they are a happy people who enjoy the pleasures of life.

Their bodies are always oily—partly from not bathing and partly from smearing them with yak butter as protection from the frost-

Tibetan yaks

Top: An evening halt of the traders.
Below: Some traders enjoying afternoon tea; the bamboo instrument used to make
the salted tea can be seen in the left of the picture.

Top: Close-up of a Tibetan tent-home.
Below: The path to God is not a smooth one. There are no roads or even footpaths here. Pilgrims must walk on these stones with utmost care, and finding the way without a guide is simply not possible.

saturated wind. Even so, during periods of intense frost, they sometimes get blisters and use *jaggery* (raw sugar) as a cure for this. The woolen cloth that covers their bodies down to the ankles is removed only when it is worn out and needs to be replaced. Sheepskin is also worn during the coldest months. The combination of animal hides, yak butter and unwashed clothes makes an unusual odor that is difficult for foreigners to get used to.

Both men and women wear the same style of clothing. The women braid their hair in a number of sections and hang shells or beads on the ends. They wear ornaments made from the horns of the musk deer and silver beads, and hang a talisman or a long string of prayer beads around the neck to ward off evil spirits. The men also have braids and wear a large ring in the left ear. It is not easy to distinguish between a man and a woman at first glance. Socially, Tibet does not seem to have been afflicted with caste distinctions. The people here are open and friendly; the *lamas* and officials are a cultured, polite and hospitable lot.

Food and Occupation

Wheat flour and raw meat are the staples of Tibetan diet, but it is the rich, thick milk and butter of the yak that are relished most. The butter, which is stored in containers made of yak hide, is also used as fuel for the lamps.

Salted tea is a popular drink in Tibet. It is made by boiling Chinese tea in water, pouring it into a bamboo container and adding butter. The mixture is then beaten thoroughly with a round piece of wood that is suitably shaped for the purpose. Salt is added to the tea, just as sugar sometimes is in other parts of the world. A Tibetan might consume 50 to 150 cups of this tea a day. On special occasions, the people drink *chang*, a beer brewed out of barley. There is no firewood in Tibet; the dung of animals is dried and used as fuel for the hearth. It is common to see women collecting dung from the open areas and putting it into baskets hanging down their backs. Later the dung is stored in heaps in the front yards. The *dama* shrub contains an oily substance that enables it to burn while it is still green, and in some areas this, too, is used for fuel. In order to conserve their precious fuel, the Tibetans dry their meat in the sun rather than cooking it.

Most Tibetans lead the life of herdsmen and women, caring for the goats and yaks. Some are traders, and some support themselves by weaving carpets and clothes from yak wool. Both men and women weave their own gloves and socks. The herdsmen live in tents, shifting them to fresh grazing lands from time to time. The tents are made out of rugs woven from yak wool. Some traders dig deep openings in the slopes of the hills, making caves in which to live. A few houses with walls and floors made of mud and rubble, and roofs made of poles, grass and shrubs, compose a village. The difficulty of transporting heavy timber from the lower Indian regions makes the construction of larger houses impossible. Tibetan monasteries are built in the same way, but these are larger in area and usually have more than one story.

Every summer, the Indian traders come into this region and barter *jaggery*, wheat, rice and other goods for the rugs and fur of the Tibetans. They move around from place to place, but their trade is almost always barter. In the past, a type of currency known as *danga* was sometimes used; if a payment less than the denomination of the currency was to be made, the coin was broken and only part of it given in payment. Neither party would be concerned about the size of a piece. How simple and trusting are the ways of these people! Of course, Chinese and Indian currency have been gradually introduced into Tibet, and both are now in circulation there.

Religion

The Tibetans are very pious people, who worship the holy image of Lord Buddha. At least one member of each family enters the order of monks and becomes a *lama*, living in a *gumfa* or monastery. Children of all ages daily recite the *mantra* "*OM Mani Padme Hum*" with great devotion. A stone plaque with this *mantra* engraved on it is buried within the boundary of every village. Piles of stones with the *mantra* engraved on them lie along the mountain paths. In the center of each pile is a tall pillar-like stone with cloths of various colors draped around it. The people walk around these stones in solemn reverence and worship there on their knees, repeating the same holy words that are written on the stones. It is believed that by circling a number of *mantras* in this way, one can achieve the benefit of repeating the *mantra* that number of times. Just observing the humble and steadfast devotion of these people as they perform their simple worship transports the person watching to the very gates of heaven.

The *lamas* shave their heads and wear brown robes. Their hearts and bodies reflect purity. During the religious celebrations in the spring, they wear silk robes and a type of headpiece. The government of Tibet is neither monarchy nor republic.* It is taken for granted that the *lamas* are the rulers here. The *lamas* have a keen and devoted interest in the country and the people they serve, and the people respect their great wisdom and dedication. Consequently, the chief *lama* of the local monastery has more or less become an absolute ruler whose orders are carried out by the officials with unquestioning obedience, while the people seek his guidance in every aspect of their daily lives. Of course, there are both men and women who become *lamas*.

This is life in Tibet as the travelers encountered it on their journey. Let us now proceed to Kailash, stopping as necessary along the Tibetan path.

---

*For at least 1,500 years, the nation of Tibet has had a complex relationship with China. In the 1950s, the Chinese government revoked most aspects of Tibet's autonomy and initiated resettlement. As of 2010, The People's Republic of China claims that Tibet is an integral part of China. The Tibetan Government-in-Exile maintains that Tibet is an independent state under unlawful occupation.

This is the long line of traders and pilgrims; it extended far beyond the eyes of the photographers or the lens of the camera.

Chapter 13

Clouds at Play

9 July. A short walk from Jangu brought us to a steep rise in our path and a view that extended for many miles. We looked out over a wide, open plain, surrounded by a fortress of high peaks. A host of soft, snow-white clouds were playing hide and seek on the surface of the peaks–now covering them, now skipping away–revealing an endless blue sky and peak after peak of the vast Himalayan range. We felt as if we had accidentally stumbled into the celestial realm, and would even have been able to see Mount Kailash, the Lord of the Himalayas, from here if it had not been for the clouds. They reminded us of the story of the divine bull Nandi who stood in front of the entrance to the temple at Chidambaram, blocking the devotee Nandan's view of Lord Siva.

A Yak Poses

We crossed the plain and reached Salthu around one in the afternoon. The white clouds suddenly turned black, showing promise of a torrential downpour. We broke journey to camp on the bank of the river and ended up staying there for the night. The following morning, Maan Singh complained that both of his mules were overtired. Another driver made a similar complaint, and both drivers asked to be paid off. We had no way of replacing them here, but still we had to let them go. We would now have only nine mules rather than twelve, and three of the mules hired for riding would be used to carry baggage instead.

The path from Salthu led us over three small hills and a plain. We crossed them all with ease that same morning and soon came to the banks of the river Sivasailam. The river was swift, clear and cold in her passage. The mules swam across with the baggage and then returned to carry us across. When we reached the other side, we pitched camp on the river bank.

Both our guide and the mule drivers warned us that once we left the banks of the Sivasailam we would not see water again for a long time. We decided to stay here for the night, since it was certain that if we did leave in the afternoon we would not be able to find water again by nightfall. We took a long bath in the river, had a leisurely lunch and spent a peaceful afternoon resting quietly in the sun. A few herds of yak grazed here and there on the narrow patches of grass around us. A black and white she yak mooed once and stood looking at us, as calm and motionless as a statue. I took this as an invitation to photograph her and did so. When dusk began to fall, the yaks slowly started to leave for some unknown destination.

His Will Was Acting

11 July, Morning. We packed up to go and sought out the mule drivers, who informed us that the mules had disappeared. The drivers knew from experience that the mules liked to go ahead at their own pace, and thought they might have gone up the path in the direction we were heading. It turned out that the drivers had guessed correctly, but it still took quite a while for them to retrieve the animals and return to camp. Consequently, the baggage did not get loaded until ten o'clock. We had been warned that we would not find water for a long time, and had planned to leave early enough to insure reaching a river again by nightfall. This morning's unscheduled events had made that impossible. Such instances served as a constant reminder that although we can always plan ahead, the Lord sometimes has a plan of His own.

We finally set out and after a long climb came to a broad plain. It was especially hot that day, and the sky was blue and cloudless. The sun beat down mercilessly on the pilgrims. I found the intense heat particularly oppressive, and soon had to rest after every step. I slowed down and let the others go on ahead. In a little while I was unable to walk at all. Even though I was now alone, I was unable to enjoy the usually-soothing quietness of solitude. Both body and spirit were spent. My heart prayed, "Oh Lord, unflagging support of this weakling, I am exhausted. Take me in Your arms." My prayers fell upon the holy ears of the Lord; I looked up to see the driver of one of the riding mules coming toward me with his animal.

The mule had been carrying Mr. Praveen until someone up ahead opened an umbrella. The sudden flash of black cloth alarmed the mule, which consequently threw its rider. Although Mr. Praveen was not hurt, he understandably declined to get back on the mule. Since I had not been seen for some time, the driver started back down the path to find me. Once again, the Lord's will was acting. My eyes saw a man coming with a mule, but my heart sang the praise of Him who relieves the suffering of His devotees. I thanked the man wholeheartedly with a great feeling of reverence for that spirit of God within him and mounted the mule.

The mule by now was tired of climbing and frustrated at being so far behind its mates; it neighed and started back up the hill at a slow pace. The driver was also tired and frustrated. I was glad that I could at least appease the driver by offering him some sweetmeats and grapes. Once we reached the peak of the hill, my heart would not let me continue to burden the animal. I had just dismounted and started walking again when the Lord of Kailash appeared before me in the distance. Just as His grace had enabled me to see His presence in the mule driver minutes before, it now enabled me to glimpse His splendor in the holy crest of Mount Kailash. My heart was filled with joy beyond expression, and I prostrated on the ground in worship. All of the fatigue of the journey vanished. All of the trials and hardships of the pilgrimage became meaningless. A joyful prayer escaped my lips: "I have seen my Father! How could I want for more? You have appeared before me. You have rid me of all pain. My heart is full. Oh Lord Siva, prostrations unto Thee! Jai Siva! Jai Siva! Jai Siva!" I forgot myself completely. The holy song of Appar Swamigal filled my heart and I found myself repeating it.

I worship Thee who is infinite like the sky, Yet appears on earth in forms for us to see.

I worship Thee, the maker of this form, Who ever abides as the formless soul within.

I worship Thee, whose compassion knows no measure, Who blesses those who suffer in His name.

I worship Thee whose riches are eternal,

The merciful King who has made my heart His throne.

I worship Thee who entered my mind in stillness, And absorbed me into His endless ocean of Peace.

I worship Thee, the destroyer of all my sins;

I worship and worship Thee, Oh my Lord of Kailash!

Looking for an Oasis

The holy vision of the Lord of Kailash was so powerful that I could scarcely bear to take my eyes away. Still, I was overwhelmed at the thought of how much more powerful this sight would be from up close. Eager to see the Lord of Kailash in His fullness and become totally immersed in that bliss, I hastily left my lookout. The vision of the Lord disappeared from view as I descended. Likewise, is it not true that we can only realize God-consciousness by scaling the spiritual heights that rise far beyond "I" and "mine?" How quickly we lose sight of Him when we descend to the lower levels of life.

I joined the others who by now had decided to stop for something to eat. The mule drivers were anxious to find a river and refused to stop, even for these few minutes. I watched the mule I had been riding as it followed its master up the hill; it reminded me of the sincere seeker with faith in his spiritual guide, who follows him unquestioningly to the goal. I quickly swallowed a few bites and left to catch up with the mule. The driver had slowed down to wait for me, and the other mules were already far ahead. He expressed displeasure at having been delayed again, but I offered no excuse as I mounted the mule. We started slowly, climbing up and down the hills, looking for a place with water where we could spend the night. It was like looking for an oasis in the desert.

Kemlung Meadows: More Lost Mules

The day's journey, which had begun at ten that morning, finally ended on the banks of the river Sutlej at seven in the evening. At one point, a sudden wind came up and the mules had huddled together. I brought both legs to one side of my mule, intending to dismount, but before I even knew what was happening, I had been thrown to the ground. Fortunately, I escaped serious injury, and after pulling a few thorns out of my arm I was ready to go again. How many times we fall and rise, fall and rise, over and over, before we finally reach the feet of the Lord! That night our group camped on the bank of the Sutlej. The next morning the drivers again complained that their mules were lost and went in search of them. Kemlung Meadows was only a mile away. The guide had already told us of a warm spring there, so we cheerfully set out to bathe while the drivers were looking for the mules. To our great disappointment, we found that the spring had dried up. We bathed in the cold water of the river instead, and awaited the arrival of the mules in one of the caves dug out of a nearby slope. By one o'clock in the afternoon the mule drivers still had not shown up. Hunger waits for no man, and we started to make some *parotta* out of the wheat flour we had brought with us. Just then the drivers arrived with the mules, and we all ate. After lunch, we were finally able to start the day's trek.

A Riverside Throne

A wooden swing bridge served as a crossing over the river Sutlej. The bridge was not strong enough to hold the mules, so the drivers and porters carried the baggage while the mules swam across the river. On the opposite shore was a milk-white formation, right at the water's edge, which looked like a throne of ivory, and we marveled at the craftsmanship of this structure. As we got closer we could see that the "throne" was actually a crystalline deposit of boracite formed at the mouth of a hot water spring. Learning that this was a natural phenomenon, however, only increased our sense of wonder. We traveled another four miles that afternoon, passing more cave dwellings along the way. The ground around them was scattered with the bones and hides of goats. A woman sat outside one of the caves, contentedly weaving socks out of yak wool. The dried dung, which was used as fuel, was piled outside another cave. The heavy smell of meat clung to the air; we found it to be quite repulsive and quickened our pace as we went by.

Gurgiyang Gumfa: A Buddhist Monastery

We walked on past the cave dwellings to Gurgiyang Gumfa. This was the first Buddhist monastery we had seen in Tibet. A tall pole with a flag flying on it welcomed us at the entrance. After climbing the many steps, we came to a spacious hall, beautifully decorated and illuminated by the glow of hundreds of oil lamps lit in rows. Both sides of the long hall were lined with long shelves of holy books. At the far end stood the elegant seat of the chief *lama*. Next to it was a round box-like table on which the *Tripitaka* sat. Carpets were laid down the length of the hall in two rows; this is where the *lamas* sat for prayer and meditation. We were awed by the beauty and sanctity of this place and looked around in wide-eyed wonder for a long time before making an offering to the chief *lama*, who lit the altar lamp. We also offered some joss sticks and colored cloths, which we had bought in Milam for this purpose. The cloths are traditionally of five colors—white, yellow, red, green and purple—and are used to decorate the holy image of the Lord. After we had made our offerings, we knelt down and prayed for the peace of the universe. A small piece of colored cloth was given to each of us as *prasad*. Yak curd was also given as *prasad*.

Tibetans and Siva Worship

At one end of the *gumfa* we saw some papers that had been painted with black ink and spread out to dry. A monk was copying sacred books onto similar black sheets with gold paste. Another monk at the other end was also copying holy writings; his work was done on white paper with silver paste.

At the rear of the hall were beautifully painted statues, so life-like that they seemed to be walking toward us. There were images of Lord Buddha and Bodhisattva and also one of Dumchak, the dancing Siva and Parvathi. In this region where the spiritual and physical worlds manifest His beauty and grace so eloquently, it was not surprising to find that people here—who are devout Buddhists—nonetheless believe in the worship of Siva and Devi, whose forms represent the unmanifested Absolute and the power of creation. The *gumfa* was like another world, and we stayed here as long as we could. When we finally descended the steps, we quickly came back to the reality of our surroundings.

Our immediate task was to find a place to set up camp. We located a spot in the plain about half a mile away and pitched our tents there. It was noon, and I put some oil on my body with the intention of bathing. Just then, a sudden gale came up with such force that it uprooted one of the tents. I postponed my bath while we refixed the stakes firmly and took shelter inside. The wind did not stop—nor the bath materialize—at all that day. When night fell, we chanted *bhajans* and retired. Shortly thereafter, the mule drivers came and demanded to be paid in full to that date. They were adamant that they should be paid immediately rather than in the morning, so we got up and paid them. When the accounts had been settled to everyone's satisfaction, we went back to bed.

Temple at Kemlung with *mantra*-carved rocks. A Tibetan state tax collector appears in the foreground.

Top: Another view of Kemlung Gumfa. A hot water spring exists here.
Below: An ivory throne on the opposite bank of the river. It turned out to be a
crystal formation made by boracite from a hot spring.

Top: Pilgrims worship at the altar in the Gurgiyang monastery.
Below: The dancing deities Siva and Parvathi, known here as Dumchak.
This statue is found in the Buddhist monastery, Gurgiyang Gumfa.

A huge statue of Lord Buddha.

Chapter 14

Coming into View of Him

14 July. We reached Thirthapuri at one in the afternoon. This is an important place of pilgrimage in Tibet; it lies on the banks of the Indus, a powerful river that originates from Manasa Sarovaram and crashes down the hills in a tumble of rushing water and rolling rocks. The monastery is the only building in Thirthapuri, and the monks are the only residents there. Near the monastery is a geyser. The water is boiling hot where the geyser erupts, but it gets cooler and cooler as it flows down the river and mixes with more and more of the water from the Indus. The point along the bank at which each pilgrim enters the river depends on how warm he likes his bath water. How wonderful it is that Mother Nature has water ready at just the right temperature for each of her children to relieve their aches and pains when they come to her for comfort. There is no gauge that can measure her love. We decided to take our time bathing in the tepid lime-mixed water, and it was noon before we left to visit the monastery. The walls of the entryway were lined with holy images of Lord Buddha, Bodhisattva and other revered souls—all beautifully painted in captivating colors. We spent the night at the monastery and awoke the next day feeling greatly refreshed.

15 July, Morning. We went to bathe again in the river and—as is the custom at a place of pilgrimage—reverently circled the boundaries of Thirthapuri before returning to the monastery for our morning prayers. A small piece of white cloth is given as *prasad* to those who worship there—a reminder that those who worship the Lord will attain a pure heart. As we were leaving, I noticed a pile of ashes and once again my imagination led me back to the time of the *Puranas*.

Basmaasura: The Undoing of a Demon

In ancient times there lived an *asura* by the name of Basmaasura, who performed intense *tapas* while worshipping Lord Siva. Because of his austerities, the Lord appeared before him. Basmaasura begged the Lord to grant him a boon, and the Lord–who never refuses the prayers of a devotee–granted it. The boon was that Basmaasura would have the power to turn anyone he touched into ash when he placed his hand over the head. The beastly *asura* immediately decided to test the power of the boon on the Lord Himself, but the Lord–sensing what was about to happen–instantly fled. The *asura* followed in pursuit.

Lord Vishnu, who had been watching all of this take place, assumed the form of a beautiful damsel and appeared before the *asura*. The *asura* immediately lost his heart to the beauty of this maiden and forgot his pursuit. He asked her to marry him and become his consort. The maiden accepted. Since there was no reason to wait, she suggested that Basmaasura should have a bath in preparation for the wedding, which could then take place at once. The *asura* looked around for some water, but he finally had to return to the maiden and tell her that he had not been able to find any. Lord Vishnu materialized a jar of water and told the *asura* that he should at least smear a little of this on his head to neaten his hair. In the midst of his passion, the *asura* lost his head as well as his heart. Forgetting the power of his boon, he took some water in his hand, and as soon as he touched his hand to his head, was instantly burned to ash.

Throughout the years, many ascetics have performed their *yagna*–holy sacrifice–in this place where the Lord appeared to Basmaasura. The pile of ashes there reminds us that though the Lord's favor might be won through devotion, a boon granted to those with evil intent only serves to bring about their own destruction. Forgetting the *asura*, but remaining immersed in thoughts of the justice and wisdom of the Lord, we departed from Thirthapuri at nine in the morning and went on to Saashak Meadows. "*Saa*" means soil and "*shak*" means ochre dye. The ochre-colored earth found here is used as a dye, and many of the people even color their cattle and goats with it as a form of decoration.

Circling His Abode

The *pradakshina*–the devotional walk around the holy peak–is an important part of the pilgrimage; it is the formal worship that takes place when the pilgrim reaches his destination. The route we would take to walk around Kailash is 32 miles long and goes up and down the slope at heights ranging from 17,000 to 19,000 feet. It is a difficult route, but there are no obstacles that cannot be surmounted by devotion and determination, and we were immersed in His ocean of divine bliss the whole time.

We crossed Saashak Meadows and reached the banks of the river Karlap by noon. This was an important part in our journey: the path leading from the Karlap would bring us into view of Mount Kailash–and to the culmination of our pilgrimage. For the next eleven days we would be blessed to be able to see the holy physical form of the Lord of Kailash, the One who has taken abode in the Himalayas with Uma Devi as His consort, and who continually bestows on His worshippers the nectar of His blessings.

We decided to set up camp on the banks of the Karlap and begin our circumambulation of Kailash the following morning. The peak of Manthatha was visible toward the south. Many years ago, a king of Manthatha had given up his crown to become a monk. He retired to the Himalayas to perform penance and attained sainthood there. The greatness of the mountain reminds us still of the greatness of that holy renunciate. The snowy cap of Manthatha mirrored the evening sun spectacularly, and we could well enjoy its radiance in spite of the distance that separated us. A giant lake of equal beauty graced its peak. This seemed an especially fitting place from which to begin our perambulation, and we used the afternoon to meditate, rest and reflect on what was about to take place.

The following morning we bathed in the Karlap and left her banks at eight. Setting my mind firmly on the goal and bearing the flower of love as my offering, I set out with our small band to worship at the holy feet of the Lord of Kailash. As we walked, we chanted the song of praise that Appar Swamigal had sung when he had seen the Lord of Kailash:

I worship Thee, the formless within all forms;

The soundless hum from which all matter comes.

I worship Thee who made the universe out of Himself;

I worship Thee who pervades it as the wind.

I worship Thee who gave the sun its brilliance;

I worship Thee who commands the fire and rain.

I worship Thee, the destroyer of all evil, Whom even the power of death cannot defeat.

I worship Thee who speaks to the hearts of His devotees, Yet need not utter any words to speak.

I worship Thee whose peace is everlasting;

I worship Thee, the victorious Lord of all.

I worship Thee who grants my every breath;

I worship and worship Thee, Oh my Lord of Kailash!

The Vision of the Lord

Now an entirely new feeling filled me. Experiencing that great Lord through just the mind and senses alone would be a ceaseless nectar for all time; but it is the experience beyond the senses–the realization of His fullness within–that brings the ultimate, unending joy! Even the most heartless and non-believing would be certain to realize the truth of His grace, if they only once had a glimpse of Him. I continued to sing His glory:

I worship Thee, the essence of all the scriptures;

I worship Thee whose praise the wise men sing.

I worship Thee who is beyond all pain and pleasure;

I worship Thee who pervades my every thought.

I worship Thee who is one without a beginning;

I worship Thee whose being never will end.

I worship Thee who is both substance and its shadow;

I worship Thee who reveals His all through grace.

I worship Thee to whom the saints pay homage;

I worship Thee, the ceaseless fount of joy.

I worship Thee who is my heart's beloved;

I worship and worship Thee, Oh my Lord of Kailash!

The *Puranas* describe Mount Kailash as a "Peak of Silver." Those who have seen Kailash in the rays of the morning sun know what this means. The mountain itself is a radiant temple of grace and beauty. What has man built throughout all of his history that can rival the works of the Divine Architect! The most impressive temples in all the world are but imperfect imitations of the perfection one sees in the *gopurams*, halls, streets and the *sanctum sanctorum* of this natural temple where the Lord's presence is seen and felt so strongly.

It is not practical to try to describe the appearance of the Lord. His divine person presents a different vision of heavenly beauty from every angle. It is no wonder that the people in this part of the world have so many names and descriptions for the Absolute: He has so many appearances and guises, and each devotee sees only the one from where he stands. The Lord who wears the Ganges on His crown appears silver. He who is covered in holy ash is white. He who has drunk poison to save His devotee from death appears blue. He also appears as black, red, orange, green and as Light itself. In the center of the peak of Mount Kailash, the Lord appears in the simplest possible form, which is called Viswalingam. Although He manifests thus in a physical form, He is surrounded by ice and snow and the devotee cannot get physically close to Him.

The *Puranas* tell that the person of the Lord is the synthesis of male and female–called Ardhanaareeswara–and that the left half of

His body is the Holy Mother. This is also seen at Mount Kailash. The eastern wing of Kailash, which appears on the left, is the *sanctum sanctorum* of the Mother Ganges. If we take time to reflect on the idea that the Mother is part of God–or that He is both male and female at once–the truth of this becomes self-evident.

Nature is a combination of *jadam*, the medium through which the essence functions, and *chaitanyam*, the all-pervading consciousness, which we also call soul or Siva. In the individual, the body is the manifestation of nature through which the soul–or God–functions. Life cannot be expressed without the body; the body has nothing to express without the soul. Ardhanaareeswara represents this principle in form; it is Siva and Shakti shown as one.

The Lord of Kailash is also known as Dakshinamoorthi. Here, under a white banyan tree, the Lord imparted knowledge through silence to King Janaka and the other devotees who sat at His feet. As soon as one sees His form in Kailash, love for Him wells up in the heart. Silence reaches and teaches him the very moment he sets his sight on the form of the Silent Teacher. The mind passes effortlessly beyond the bounds of time and becomes immersed in the boundless grace of God. That joy of knowing that the seer, the seeing and the seen are One is experienced.

He who has once seen the glow of the Lord will live in that happiness all of his life. How can we ascribe one color, one shape, one quality to the Lord of the world who is far beyond the colors, shapes and qualities of the world He created? The omnipresent Lord is not one whom we can limit with our imagination. Yet He chooses to be the simple companion of the selfless devotee and so appears to him in various guises and disguises.

He appears golden throughout the dawn and silver in the hot noon-time sun. In the evening, He appears emerald. The clouds that wind their way through the sky flow down over His shoulder like a river. All of these heavenly sights are fleeting images that pass within a few moments. We enjoyed them all with His blessings, and soon reached the path that would lead us around His holy abode.

Landi Gumfa: The Lord is in Front and Behind

The noontime sun was intense, but the Lord provided the feet of the pilgrims with a carpet of cool green grass, which He had decorated in flowers of various shades. We walked leisurely along this soft garden path and soon came to the monastery of Landi Gumfa. What a beautiful hall we entered there! We worshipped the images by lighting lamps before them and walked around to see this very ancient monastery.

What a surprise to discover the Lord of Kailash standing in front of us—when we had just seen Him in the opposite direction. We walked toward this second image, and found that we were actually looking into a mirror where we saw the image of the Lord as Kailash Peak being reflected—just as His image is reflected in the pure hearts of His devotees. We lit the lamps before the mirror image and joyfully paid homage to the Lord again, worshipping the light of His love and singing His glory.

Dorafuk Gumfa: Some Quiet Moments with Him

We walked on to Dorafuk Gumfa that same day. There we dispersed in different directions for the evening. Some meditated, others rested. I looked for a solitary spot where I could sit before the Lord of Kailash and bask—alone and uninterrupted—in His beauty. I found a peaceful, quiet place and sat as motionless as a statue. The peak that reflects the glorious light of the Absolute appeared before me in an array of colors that changed every moment in the reflected light of the sun. My heart swelled at the sight of His radiance. I could think only of Him. The Lord had so totally captured my heart that I decided I had to capture His image on film. I took out my camera and looked through the lens— only to find that His holy image was gone! I looked up, but the Lord of Kailash had disappeared. Was I dreaming? I did not think so. Perhaps our playful Lord was only hiding from me behind a veil of clouds. I decided to wait for Him to reappear, certain that He would do so.

A long time passed, but still I waited. I made a firm resolve not to move until I had seen Him again. My mind became more and more distressed as the time passed, but I consoled myself by thinking of the great devotees who suffered so much to have his *darshan*. How the Lord had showered His blessings upon those faithful devotees! For the first time, I fully understood the meaning of the saying, "Who can see Him, if He decides not to reveal Himself?" (Appar Swamigal, *Thevaram*).

At last the Lord decided to bless me, too, with His kindness. He appeared before me once again as He had earlier. I worshipped Him, photographed Him three times and worshipped Him again. Darkness started to slowly close in, and my friends began to return, one by one, bringing my solitude to an end.

The Holy Mount of Kailash, where Siva, the Lord of the Universe, dwells.

Chapter 15

Stories of Mount Kailash

We were glad to be able to meet with the chief *lama* while at Dorafuk Gumfa. Although we only spoke for a short while, he gave us some new insights into the deep and abiding reverence that the Tibetans feel toward Kailash. These are some of the things he told us:

Kailash is known to the Tibetans as Gangarin Poshi. The Tibetans are devout followers of the Buddhist faith, and—for many hundreds of years–this has been a holy place of pilgrimage for them. Many Buddhist monks have performed penance and attained *nirvana* here.

Physically, the peak of Kailash resembles a Buddhist monastery, and, in fact, four Buddhist monasteries have been built around it. The *lamas* there perform prayers and religious rituals in reverence to Mount Kailash daily. They do not solicit money from pilgrims for performance of the rites, but they do accept any donations made to help cover expenses.

God is seated on Kailash in the form known as Dumchak, or Siva. His hair is matted, and He wears a tiger skin. He also carries a drum and trident (*trisulam*). He is flanked by Shakti, who is called Kanto. Lord Buddha lives on the peak with many hundreds of Bodhisattvas. The divine beings stroll around the mountaintop where celestial music–which can be heard by sincere devotees of God–continuously rings in the air.

The *lamas* repeat the sacred *mantras* and worship God day and night. During certain auspicious times, they pay reverence to Mount Kailash by uninterrupted singing of its glory for long intervals. The

Tibetan government also takes a keen interest in the worship here. The Tibetan people are filled with great joy when the spring sets in. As the sun melts the snow, the path around Kailash opens to them. They walk the 32 miles around the peak 51 times within a given period, praying the whole time. This is considered to be the most pious form of worship.

Pradakshina with Full Prostrations

Other devotees cover the distance around Kailash with full prostrations in a practice known as *sasthaanga pradakshina*. This amazing feat is done across the same 32 miles of snow, glaciers, hills and rocky slopes ordinarily covered on foot. The devotees first worship Mount Kailash in the light of dawn. Then they set out with a few woolen blankets and a lunch parcel, which will be their only possessions during the pilgrimage. When they have walked the distance they think they can cover by *sasthaanga pradakshina* before nightfall, they put down the parcels and return to the place from which they started that morning. Here they clasp their hands over their heads and pray to the Lord of Kailash. When they come to the end of the prayer, they stretch themselves out full-length on the ground with their arms overhead, their hands clasped in worship. A mark is made on the ground where the tips of their fingers touch. Then they stand up, walk in prayer to the mark and repeat the ritual. They proceed in this way until sunset and then spend the night on the path. The same procedure is again followed the next morning. The entire worship takes 28 days. Such a feat is possible for these devotees because of their unfaltering determination and absolute faith. The penance has been performed since time immemorial.

This unrivaled penance had us amazed. It shows how very holy the Buddhists consider Mount Kailash to be. The Hindus attest that by performing penance at Kailash one may attain the feet of Siva, while the Buddhists affirm that one may attain *nirvana* there. If we look beyond the different terms used by the Hindus and Buddhists into the experiences of both, we will realize the truth that the final goal of all religions is in fact the same. The difference is only in the names and not in the Absolute. Whoever attempts to attain His divine grace will attain it. Are not all of His children equal in His kingdom?

An Ancient Story: Ravana's Desire

Stories and fables about Kailash abound, illustrating every principle expressed in its holy form. For instance, the Tibetans tell that Ravana, the King of Lanka–who was strong and famous in the world of *asuras* (demons)–performed penance on the shores of the Giant Lake near the peak of Kailash for a long period, and so was blessed by the Lord. Once bestowed with the Lord's grace, a new idea came to his mind. He decided to uproot Mount Kailash and plant it in his own country of Lanka. He shoved the stick he was carrying into the ground at the base of Mount Kailash, threw a rope around the peak and pulled. Mother Parvathi shook with fear as the mountain quaked. The Lord pressed down with his toe, and Ravana–caught under the peak–yelled out with pain. As Ravana began to realize the superior strength of the Lord, he began to sing His glory. Siva then released the demon, who returned to Lanka. The Tibetans maintain that the pillar-like form seen in Kailash to this day is the stick of Ravana. Further, they say that the ridges on the slopes of Kailash–which can be seen in the photograph in this book–are the marks made by his rope when he lassoed the peak.

Ravana's Anger

According to the Hindu version of the story, the Pushpak plane of Ravana was able to traverse all the corners of the three worlds unhindered and would instantly transport him wherever he wanted to go. Ravana had vanquished all of the *devas,* including Indra, Vishnu and Brahma, and had also defeated the mighty Kubera whose kingdom was in the Kailash ranges. He now looked around for new realms to conquer. Kailash stood before him. Ravana commanded it to make way for his plane, but the peak stood silent and motionless. The *asura* king was furious and so decided to uproot the peak with his powerful hands. The peak shook, the orderlies of the Lord shivered with terror. Mother Parvathi clung tightly to her Lord. The Lord, in order to save them all from destruction, pressed down with his toe, crushing Ravana beneath the peak. Shamed by his defeat and tormented with pain, the *asura* yelled to be heard throughout all of creation. Appar Swamigal has beautifully narrated this incident in verse:

Seeing Kailash rich in gold,
Diamonds, pearls and emeralds, old,
Mighty Ravana—bold and brave—
Shifted alone the mountain great.
Uma in fright her Lord embraced,
Press did He His holy foot and
Crushed the demon in great distress.
Who can face Lord Siva's wrath?

Ravana's shouting made the angels in the skies tremble. The seas rose and fell. The peak shook. The Lord's entourage of *siddhas* (highly evolved souls) wondered what was happening. All of life shivered with the fear that the end of the world was at hand. At last one of the saints, who pitied Ravana's suffering, reminded him that the Lord loves to hear the songs of the *Sama Veda*. On hearing this, the *asura* finally realized that singing the glory of the Lord was the only way to salvation, and so sang His praise for a period of 1,000 years. The Lord, full of compassion for the repenting *asura* king, blessed him with long life and gifted him with a sword that would overcome all foes.

The Moral of the Story

Who is this demon Ravana? Some say he is a tyrant who exhibits only the basest qualities and is totally unworthy of any consideration. This is a mistake. If we look at the story without any bias, we will be able to see something of Ravana's life in our own. This King of Lanka is the great grandson of Brahma. Brahma is the power of creation whose son is Pulasthiar, the perfect being. Brahmarishi is the perfect son of Pulasthiar. Ravana is the son of Brahmarishi. Because of his high birth, Ravana shines in learning, broadness of mind and faith in God.

When the soul manifests, first the faculty of bliss takes shape, followed by the faculty of wisdom and then the faculty of mind. Brahma is the soul. His son Pulasthiar is the faculty of bliss, Brahmarishi is the wisdom born of bliss and Ravana is the mind born of wisdom. The relationship of Brahma and Ravana is the same as that of the mind and the soul. The mind is the offspring of the soul. The moment the mind thinks of an object, it takes the shape of that object. That is why Ravana can take any form he desires. Ravana also has ten heads. This symbolizes that the mind acts through the five senses of cognition and the five senses of action.

The epics record that Ravana, having performed penance for 10,000 years, ruled the three worlds. The lesson learned from his life is that by performing penance with single-minded devotion, control of the very nature comes within one's reach. When the mind is fortified by penance, it holds sway over every corner of the earth. With this power, one can control every atom of the universe, and change place or form at will. A mind that acquires this power, however, swells with ego and thinks that it is unequalled. If–goaded by ego–it forsakes or attempts to destroy the Absolute, which is the very source of its power, it is certain to learn its mistake through suffering. It is this principle that is conveyed when Ravana is caught under the peak. We also learn that one attains endless joy, not through the power of the mind, but by surrendering that power at the feet of the Lord without reservation. Thus, Ravana finds salvation by praying to the Lord who is his very life and strength.

Kailash of the South

When hearing the name of Ravana, the people of Lanka will also be reminded of the Kailash of the south. The Southern Kailash is found on the northeast coast of Sri Lanka at Trincomalee, a place washed by the waters of the Indian ocean and richly blessed by nature.

There is an ancient story–which has been handed down for countless generations–about Thirukonaachalam, known as Trincomalee (the name given by Western invaders), the Kailash of the South. It goes like this. Once upon a time Lord Siva was seated in North Kailash with his consort, the holy Shakti. From there he blessed Brahma, Vishnu and Indra and the other *devas* who paid him homage. He told them, "O *Devas*, Brahma's vocation shall be creation, Vishnu's duty shall be to protect, Rudra shall be the lord of destruction and Adisesha's duty shall be to bear the burden of the mass of the world." The lord of wind, Vayu, prayed to the Lord and implored, "O Lord, is Adisesha more powerful than I, who travels the fourteen worlds?" Angered by this, Adisesha retorted, "O lord of wind, what power have you who art the mere air that I breathe?" The enmity between the two grew more and more bitter until at last they prepared to settle the matter with a duel. The *devas* arranged the test of might. Adisesha was to cover all the peaks of Kailash with his hood, and the lord of wind had to try to pull out at least one peak with his strength alone. Adisesha encircled Kailash from its base to its crown, and covered it with his hood. Vayu, the lord of wind, let out all his force. The entire universe trembled with fear. The *devas* themselves sought refuge at the feet of the Lord, They told Him of the danger that the whole universe was in because of this rivalry and implored His grace.

Lord Siva, in response to their prayers, ordered Brahma to create another abode for Him on Thirukona Peak in the southern part of North Kailash. He took a seat on this peak with the Mother of the Universe and whispered to Adisesha, "O Sesha! Come here. . .I want to tell you a secret!" As Adisesha bent one of his ten thousand heads closer to hear what the Lord had to say, the lord of wind plucked away the Thirukona peak as well as two others that were near it. The Lord ordered Vayu to deposit one of the peaks in the Thondai Kingdom, the second in the Chola Kingdom and the Thirukona Peak in Eela Kingdom by the ocean. Thus, Thirukona, the seat of the Lord, was placed on the eastern coast of Sri Lanka. From then on this was called South Kailash or Thirukoneswaram. The peak placed in the Thondai Kingdom came to be known as Thirukalahasthi and that placed in the Chola Kingdom as Thiruchirappali.

Top: A frozen river.
Below: Pilgrims crossing it.

Top: An icy walk on the way to Gowri Kund at 18,000 feet.
Below: Gowri Kund: frozen banks and a blanket of ice.

Chapter 16
The Peak of Silver

18 July, Morning. We joyfully witnessed the divine dance of the sun's lively rays as it slowly rose over the horizon, and prayed to the Lord that He might bless us this day with the successful completion of our *pradakshina* and a bath in Gowri Kund. The path was quite easy at first, but soon became very rugged. Nevertheless, we continued to climb with great enthusiasm, repeating the holy name of Lord Siva with each step. Fatigue would not be able to subdue us this day.

As we walked, we noticed that the path ahead was strewn with tiny balls of silver. We were immediately reminded of the saintly Appar and how he had once been tested for non-attachment. Precious gems had been cast into the area around the temple he was cleaning until all of the temple grounds were completely covered. Appar had remained unmoved, his mind and heart centered on the even more precious feet of his beloved Lord. We wondered at first whether these silver balls had been thrown here to test us. As it turned out, however, they were not silver balls at all–but snow balls! This place is often beset by hailstorms. At times the stones can be as large as apricots, and many people have met their death in a heavy downpour. By His grace the sun was shining this day, and we were spared any such danger.

The sky was clear and blue, and the entire expanse around us sparkled with points of silver light in the unobstructed rays of the brilliant sun. The snow-covered ground looked like a field of glistening white flowers. As we climbed, our feet broke through the surface of the snow with a crunching sound. The distant slopes shone like melted silver, and our eyes suffered in the dazzling glare of the sun's reflection in spite of our dark glasses. Several members of the group became faint. We stopped to steady ourselves, climbed on to the Dolmak Pass and crossed it.

Above the pass we could see the peak where legend tells us that Kubera, the wealthy king who was subdued by Ravana, once lived. When we reached the summit of the peak at 19,000 feet, we had covered a distance of four steep miles. This was the highest point of the entire journey. We would be descending again to reach Gowri Kund. The surface of the path was very slippery because of the icy snow. We moved ahead cautiously, one step at a time. One slip and we were sure to slide all the way down into the frozen lake. Placing our spiked staffs firmly on the ground and our minds firmly on the Lord, we continued. It took great effort, but with the Lord's grace we finally reached Gowri Kund.

Gowri Kund

We stopped and stood in awe in front of the frozen lake. Gowri Kund spread before us like a sheet of glass. She was surrounded by icy peaks. We watched as a huge blanket of ice slid down one of the slopes and into the lake, breaking through the glass-like surface of snow. The peak that shed this giant ice crystal is known as Parvathi. It is only during the hottest hours of the day, when the sun is at its zenith, that one can even consider bathing in the waters of Gowri Kund. The unbearable cold provides the pilgrim with direct experience of the truth that the body and soul are indeed separate entities.

When these aspects of the bath are considered, one cannot help but wonder whether he wants to bathe in the Gowri after all. Nevertheless, I stood firm in my resolve that the pilgrimage to Kailash would not be complete until I had bathed in these holy waters, and started to prepare myself. The clouds dispersed at the very moment, and the intense heat of the sun fell directly upon us. These were God's blessings indeed. How can we express the kindness of the Divine Mother? Our joy was beyond words. I was filled with thoughts of praise and gratitude.

Bathing Amidst the Ice

We hammered the sheet of ice with a staff and looked at the cold water below. Some performed the bath mentally. One of the pilgrims walked into the water and immediately lost consciousness. He was pulled out, dried with a towel and rubbed with a woolen blanket. Within a very short time his body was warm, and he regained consciousness. Some had one dip in the water. This single dip itself was a great accomplishment, and each devotee glowed as if he were coming out of the ocean of love of the Divine Mother. Swami Premanandaji, a very hardy soul, stayed in for many dips.

I was very fortunate to be able to dip once in worship of the Lord, a second time on behalf of all devotees and a third for the welfare of the world. It was not possible to do more, and I came out onto the shore.

This bath is not just a symbolic act, and we all felt the blessings of the Divine Mother. When we came out of the water, we began to sing her praises:

O Mother, I worship Thee, I worship Thee, the goddess of Kailash.

I worship Thee, the destroyer of all past sins.

I worship Thee, the giver of every gift.

I worship Thee who shatters the illusion of birth and death.

I worship Thee who manifests as the holy river.

I worship Thee who caresses me like a mother.

I worship Thee who blesses us Her children.

I worship Thee who are my heart's beloved.

O Mother of Life, the Light of Love and Compassion,

I worship Thy blessed feet; glory and glory unto Thee!"

At the end, we prostrated again and again in worship of her.

Kailash: The Holy Land

One who treads the soil of Kailash knows that he is a blessed soul. No one could possibly reach this place on his own. Only those who have done great penance can win the grace of the Lord's strength which enables one to achieve such a goal. Once one has seen His beautiful person in the peaks of the Himalayas, the inner divine power that has been lying dormant begins to function. The mind concentrates effortlessly; one attains the stage of being able to achieve all that he desires. The worship we did upon reaching Kailash was spontaneous. The air here is filled with the sacred *mantras* and prayers repeated by *rishis* and devotees for thousands of years. These holy vibrations penetrate the mind and bring an incomparable pleasure: that supreme joy of being alive and awake in a garden filled with divine blessings, where one can sit in the shade of His holy feet and drink from the eternal spring of divine love. That feeling can only be known by experiencing it oneself.

The Power of Penance

The divine power that has created all we see around us has no attributes of its own. Anything and everything can be achieved through it. The merciful Lord listens to the prayers of all. He who prays at the feet of the Lord reaps according to his nature. One of pure mind will seek good and achieve good. One of impure mind will seek evil and achieve evil. The Lord's strength, like His grace, does not know good or bad, like or dislike, pain or pleasure. His power is like the power of electricity. Electricity is always neutral. If a fan is plugged into the power source, it makes a breeze and brings comfort. If a radio is plugged in, it provides music and brings pleasure. If a bulb is plugged in, it brings light. If a finger is plugged in, it brings a shock. Divine power is also like that. The *devas* performed penance in Kailash, and the good results were in keeping with their nature. The *asuras* performed penance, and the results were in keeping with their nature. That is the greatness of penance. Through penance one is sure to win the Lord's grace to do with as he pleases. That is why the wise choose union with Him–which brings the highest joy–as their goal. The great Tamil saint Thiruvalluvar also spoke of the power of penance. He said:

Since the prayers of the penitent are always answered, the wise will attempt penance in this life.

As the fire purifies and burns the gold, the endurance of the burning pain of austerities makes people shine.

Coming Down

Like all other experiences on this earth, pilgrimage to Kailash must also come to an end; it cannot continue indefinitely. We reached the foot of the holy peak, circled it in reverence and bathed in the holy waters of Gowri Kund. We received the Lord's blessings from the bounty of His grace. And now, it was time to begin the return journey. The inner experience, however, is one that can never be lost; our minds remained at the apex of joy as we slowly started back down the slope.

The path leading down from this point proved a steep and cold descent. Hard snow had fallen. In places the snow had cracked, leaving broad crevasses and the dangers that go with them. Further on, the path improved somewhat and continued eastward along the banks of the river. By evening we had reached Jentalfuk Gumfa. The ground around this monastery was thickly covered with a fragrant plant, which is dried and used as incense, appropriately called "Incense of Kailash." We spent the night at this monastery.

Dharchan

19 July, Morning. At 7 a.m. the rest of the group set out on the bypath to Gnyandang Gumfa. I chose to go straight to Dharchan with the mule drivers instead. Rain and cold attacked in turn along the way, and we did not reach Dharchan until 11 a.m. I set up the tent and rested inside. By this time I was quite hungry. I had some *parotta* with *jaggery*, but it was cold and damp, and what I really wanted was some hot tea. After a while the heavy rain turned to drizzle, and I peeped out of the tent. For a moment I felt as if I were in the middle of the ocean: the tent was completely surrounded by a vast expanse of water. I settled back inside and waited for the rain to stop before going out to see the village of Dharchan. There was only one building in the village, and it stood out prominently. The only other structures here were the tents that the barter traders of Milam and Tibet had put up that spring. This type of temporary trading village is called a *mandy*.

The elevation at Dharchan is 16,000 feet; those taking the Garbiang route to Kailash begin and end their *pradakshina* here. It soon started to rain again, and I returned to the tent. Within a short time I had a visitor: Swami Mukthanandaji from Rishikesh. Although we had never met before, he had seen me at Sivananda Ashram, where he lived in the garden, and had recognized me at once when I arrived in Dharchan. Although Swamiji still observed a vow of silence, which he had taken years before, he was easily able to introduce himself without speaking. He also offered me some tea with milk. My longing for tea was thus delightfully and unexpectedly fulfilled. When the rest of my group arrived from Gnyandang Gumfa, we all went out to look around the bazaar with Swami Mukthanandaji.

The Affectionate King

Swamiji led us to the palace of the king. When you hear the word "palace," however, you should not immediately think of Mysore or Versailles. This palace turned out to be the two-story building of mud and rubble that had been the only permanent structure seen among the tents on my tour of the village. The king saw Swami Mukthanandaji coming and welcomed us with a broad smile. The queen was a virtuous lady, well-suited to her position, who received the monks with great reverence, and we were all served with generous amounts of salted tea. Every year the king and the queen lived in Dharchan for six months, from April to September. Dharchan and an expanse of a few miles around it belonged to the kingdom of Bhutan. The king was legally appointed by the Bhutan government to collect taxes from the *mandy* of traders and to attend to other activities of state in the area. The traders of Milam arranged a *satsang* that night in the palace temple. Swami Premanandaji gave a discourse in Hindi on the worship of God, and I was asked to close the program with *shanti* chanting.

20 July, Morning. Our group awoke well-rested and beaming with joy. The pious pride of having accomplished the holy walk around Mount Kailash shone on all the faces. The whole group—including the mule drivers—celebrated with a grand feast. The royal couple also participated. This was the first time that the king of the palace had been entertained by pilgrims of the tent. Does it matter whether we live in palaces or tents as long as we are united by the bonds of affection?

Gnyandang Gumfa

After a short rest I decided to visit the Gnyandang Gumfa, which my fellow travelers had seen the day before. Swami Mukthanandaji accompanied me to the monastery. It was a continuous climb of about three miles to our destination. There was a flight of steps in front of the *gumfa,* with a dog guarding the monastery at each step. These dogs were not shy about baring their teeth to strangers, and we hesitated to come any closer. The guards quickly calmed the dogs, however, and sent us up to the room of the *lama.* The *lama* was a very young and wealthy man, who received us with kindness and enthusiasm. He served us salted tea from a pot that stood by his side, continually refilling the beautiful wooden cups as we spoke. We were also given some curd from goat's milk, sweetened with sugar. When the *lama* had graciously filled us with satisfying food and elevating thoughts, he escorted us down to the temple.

The Temple

This temple was even more grand than those we had seen previously. Divinity and holiness pervaded the air. We worshipped at the altar and, with the *lama's* permission, I took a few photographs. Afterward we returned to his room and resumed our conversation. The opening in the walls of the *gumfa* gave us a broad view of the area. It was a beautiful sight to see Rakshas Taal on one side and Manasa Sarovaram on the other, and at the horizon the Manthatha hills as the boundary. We continued our visit in the midst of this spectacular view. Language was an obstacle to discussion at very great length, but the language of the heart knows no obstacles and the communication of our hearts was deep and full.

We arrived at the *gumfa* at three in the afternoon and stayed until five in the evening. The *lama* saw us off with gifts of "Kailash Incense" and *prasad* from the temple. It was now getting dark, so we proceeded rather quickly to Dharchan. When we arrived, we had dinner and retired for the night. On the way, I picked up a stone that caught my eye and later arranged to have the Tibetan Buddhist *mantra, "OM Mani Padme Hum,"* engraved on it.

[*Author's note, added in 1984*: I still have the stone on my altar, even to this day. A piece of it was put into the foundation of the Light Of Truth Universal Shrine at Yogaville, Virginia. I never thought that a part of Kailash would come to the great country of the United States of America. Nothing is impossible when the Lord wants it.]

Top: Those who steadied their minds and dipped in the icy cold waters of Gowri Kund quickly covered their bodies.
Below: The palace and tents that make up the village of Dharchan.

Top left: The chief *lama* of Gnyandang Gumfa and the author.
Top right: Lord Buddha's image found in rock amidst layers of stones.
Below: Swami Mukthanandaji, the royal family representing Bhutan, Praveen and
Ramdas with the author. The Kailash peak is visible in the background.

An open invitation to peace and calm: meditation at the bank of Manasa Sarovaram.

Chapter 17

Manasa Sarovaram: The Lake of Snow

21 July, Morning. We said farewell to our Dharchan friends and started out uphill. There was a plain stretching for 10 or 12 miles beyond the peak in front of us, but we had to climb the peak in order to reach the plain. The slope seemed endless as we trudged on and on. Our legs finally refused to go any farther, and we camped on the banks of a river, pitching our tent so that we would be facing Kailash.

The next morning we started walking again, and at last arrived at the edge of the plain. The calm Manasa Sarovaram that stands between Kailash and Manthacha came into view across the plain. We started walking toward it, passing many miles of marshlands, pastures, shrubs, brooks and wild horses before reaching the shore. There we drank in the beauty of Lake Manasa. After walking along her banks for a few more miles, to rid ourselves of fatigue, we bathed happily in her waters and had something to eat.

Manasa Sarovaram lies 20 miles to the southeast of Mount Kailash at an elevation of 15,000 feet. It covers an area of about 200 square miles. The surface of the lake is completely still. It looks like a sheet of pale green glass. These glass-like waters reflect a crystal-clear image of Mount Kailash. Eight Buddhist monasteries are situated around the 54-mile circumference of the lake. The *lamas* of these monasteries have set aside specific times for the regular worship of both Mount Kailash and Manasa Sarovaram.

The surface of the lake is so still that you could watch for hours and never see a single ripple in the water. Yet its appearance continuously changes under the golden rays of the sun by day and the cooling rays of the moon by night. The fascination of Manasa Sarovaram goes much deeper than this, however. It has the power to subdue the thoughts, making the mind as calm and serene as its own surface.

Manasa is possibly the most beautiful lake on earth and universally revered as one of the holiest.

Manasa Sarovaram—so broad, so deep and so still—reminds one of a Yogi seated in deep meditation. Manasa is also called Anavathaptha. Anavathaptha means "that which is warm and motionless." Although the lake appears to be shallow, in places it is as deep as 250 feet. Nevertheless, there are many geysers below the surface, and the waters here are quite warm.

The Wonder Lotus

Lake Manasa is filled with the "wonder lotus" often referred to in Buddhist literature. The Tibetans say that Lord Buddha comes to sit among these flowers. Perhaps it is due to the touch of his feet that the wonder lotus spreads such divine light all around. Many birds live in flocks here. Among them is a species known as the royal swan, which the Tibetans revere as the "divine bird" or nangba. They listen to the sweet voice of the swans with great delight, considering it to be celestial music.

We marveled at the rainbow colors that appeared in bars across the sands of Manasa; it is almost as if the creator had used this shoreline as a pallette to mix his tints and hues. The entire lake is surrounded by a gallery of colorful works of art, painted by the greatest Master of them all.

The four rivers that irrigate the subcontinent of India—the Sindhu, Brahmaputhra, Karnali and Sutlej—arise near Lake Manasa as individual springs in the north, east, south and west respectively. Manasa Sarovaram has a special place among the pleasures of the Kailash pilgrimage. When one enters its waters, the body is purified and the mind becomes clear and still. In the midst of this calmness, love and devotion naturally spring and bubble. It would not be unjustified to call Manasa "the lake that makes one who bathes in its water divine." The men bathing here worship with tharpanam—an offering to the departed ancestors—while the women worship with offerings of incense and light.

Top: A view of Kailash. A stupa of a monastery appears in the foreground.

Below: A small beautiful statue of Dumchak, or Siva/Shakti.

Gowri Sankaran: Bliss and Mosquitoes

Pilgrims also perform *pradakshina* here, walking the entire distance around the lake. A number of rivers have to be crossed en route; but in the calming, holy atmosphere of Manasa this is not difficult at all. It is the removing of oneself from this atmosphere that is difficult. Here the worshipper becomes totally absorbed in the forms of Siva and Shakti.

These forms of God, expressed as Manasa Sarovaram and Kailash, are together known as Gowri Sankaran. We, too, walked around this holy lake and had many holy experiences there. Once the mind has become purified, it can easily feel the presence of the *siddhas* and receive their blessings.

We passed several small rivers by an assortment of bridges over the first three miles; at that point, however, we encountered a river without a bridge. We attempted to cross it anyway, but failed. We walked farther along the bank and tried again. Again we failed. Walking still farther along the bank, we suddenly found ourselves swarmed by literally millions of black mosquitoes. Every inch of mule, baggage and pilgrim was covered with a thick coat of them. The mules tried to chase them with their tails, the humans with their hands. The insects, however, were completely undeterred and firmly stood their ground. It was now two o'clock in the afternoon, and our spirits were wilted. We decided we had gone far enough for one day and set up camp.

Just then a swift gust of wind came up, filling the air with sand and dust. The mosquitoes vanished as suddenly as they had appeared—without leaving a single one of their company behind. At the same time, our tent collapsed with a bang! We found a spot to repitch the tent where the force of the wind would be less intense. Our annoyance at these problems was heightened by the fact that the guide had brought us down the wrong path. If we had taken the proper path, we would probably have been able to cross the river with ease. However, we gradually became reconciled to the day's events, which after all had provided us with a rare experience, and passed a pleasant evening.

The Mules Disappear Again

23 July, Morning. When we were ready to start the day's journey, we looked around for the mules—only to find that they had disappeared

again. We became more and more restless while waiting for them to return. Still, the shores of Manasa offered an open invitation to peace and calm. I walked towards the lake. Endless beauty stretched before me. The snow-white swans glided through the water, contentedly pecking at the lotus flowers, whose open petals sheltered the younger birds from the heat of the sun. Drops of water glistened like pearls on the lotus leaves. I was reminded of a verse written by the great Tamil poetess Aavayar almost 2,000 years ago:

> *The great and the good, full well they know*
> *In whatever way they contemplate,*
> *The body frail has ills galore:*
> *Disease and death, many and more,*
> *Live like water on a lotus leaf.*

The stillness of the pale green lake, the silent motion of the swans amidst the flowers and the calmness that filled the air restored my mind to a state of tranquility. Totally absorbed in this effortless peace, I experienced Kailash as Siva and Manasa as Shakti. The thought of lost mules was totally forgotten in this divine bliss. When true peace is experienced, there can be no anxiety over the unfolding of life. How can one worry about the world when he is in the presence of the One who created it? After enjoying this blissful state for some time, I returned to the camp.

Around 11:00 in the morning, we decided to send Divan Singh and one of the drivers back to Dharchan with a request to the king for the loan of some mules. On the way, they found our mules coming toward camp and returned with them instead. I asked one of the drivers why the mules had gone back in the direction from which we had come; he told me that they had been looking for the rich pasture they had enjoyed the previous day.

The Tibetans Also Observe The Pilgrims

Because we had gone the wrong way, we also went back in the direction from which we had come, crossing six narrow rivers in the process. At 6:00 in the evening we finally pitched our tents near the camp of some Tibetans. Our neighbors soon gathered around the cooking tent where Divan Singh was busily at work. They watched in amazement as the kerosene stove burned and buzzed, and discussed this in their own language. All of our acts seemed novel and amusing to them. Since we did not want to offend them, we refrained from asking them to leave. Eventually they went to bed, and so did we.

24 July. The next morning we left along the shores of Manasa. At 4:00 in the afternoon we reached one end of the lake, and continued walking on to Dachchu, where we came to yet another river. Here we debated whether to cross the river that night, or wait until morning. Generally, we did not attempt to cross the mountain rivers in the evenings, when they were swollen with melted snow. Swami Premanandaji, however, was not one to hesitate; he settled the debate by marching boldly forward to cross. The rest of us followed. Soon we were all caught in a torrential downpour, and hastened to the other shore where we pitched the tent and took cover. By this time we were soaked through, and so were our clothes and bedding. Having no alternative, we stretched out on wet beds. True tiredness only requires sleep—not comfort—and sleep we did.

Tokkar Gumfa: Some Novel Housing

25 July, Morning. We left Dachchu early and reached Tokkar Gumfa by 12:00 noon. The houses here were very unique. Numerous walls of rubble and mud plaster stood around the area. The traders could instantly convert these houses at any time by spreading canvas "roofs" over them. The resulting houses provided ample shelter from both sun and rain. The wooden cups and fly whisks found here were especially attractive, and we bought several. That same evening we reached the other end of Manasa and set up camp on her shore. Since we would no longer have the good fortune to bathe in this lake after the next day, we dipped again in her holy waters.

Top: Winding up a day's camp.
Below: A typical way to spend the night.

120

Top: It's all snow! No wonder it's called "Temple of Snow."
Below: Another terrain for the pilgrims to cross.

Chapter 18

Playing in the Mother's Lap

26 July. It was with great reluctance that we left the shores of Lake Manasa. Once we started climbing the steep path, however, our minds again became fully absorbed in spectacular beauty. The majestic Manthatha now stood before us.

Manthatha, with its glistening blanket of white snow, stands opposite Mount Kailash, looking very much like a mirror image of that holy peak. There are places on Manthatha where many saints have performed penance. A cave at the summit is especially revered; the *Puranas* tell that Lord Ganesh and Lord Muruga, the divine sons of Siva and Parvathi, presented their first appearance in the world from this cave.

We were able to see both Manasa Lake and Rakshas Taal as we walked across the slopes of Manthatha. The road to Dharchan was also visible from here. Kurla peak shone in the distance like a green emerald; within three hours we had reached it. Descending from there, we came to Gowri cave. The Karnali river, a tributary of the Brahmaputhra, begins its course from a point near this cave. From here the river runs through numerous canals, like a child playing in the lap of Mother Nature. We pitched our camp on the bank of the river and enjoyed the beauty of the Mother ourselves. Even at night, the scenery here is something to behold.

The Sun and the Rain Take Turns

27 July, Morning. When we had folded our tents and were ready to leave, everyone looked around and asked the now familiar question, "Where are the mules?" The animals had strayed again, and again the drivers went—grumbling—in search of them. Meanwhile, it started to rain heavily, and continued until eight o'clock. The sunshine that

followed was bright and hot. What sudden changes! The rain and sun continued to alternate with each other all day long, just as pain and pleasure alternate throughout all of one's life.

Lunch time arrived, but the mules did not. We ate, and resumed our waiting. It was four o'clock in the afternoon when the animals finally showed up. We quickly packed–pacifying the dejected drivers as best we could–and started out. Thorny bushes grew thickly along the path. These were covered with clusters of the most beautiful flowers. We carefully found our way down the steep slope and pitched the tent next to a brook not far from the Karnali. The light drizzle that greeted us turned into a heavy rain and continued until midnight.

Takla Fort

28 July. We started out at 8:00 in the morning and reached Takla Fort around 1:00 p.m. The fort is located at 12,000 feet on the Tibetan plateau, within the Broong valley. This is the largest village in Tibet, and a very beautiful one. The land was green as far as the eye could see. The waters that rushed down the mountains and spread out in many canals shared their abundance with the hungry crops–mainly wheat and peanuts–which grew green and lush all around. A few tall trees stood out prominently among the widely-spaced houses.

On the summit of a peak in Takla Fort is a temple dedicated to the Lord in the form of the Siva Lingam. To reach it, one has to cross the river Karnali and climb a steep slope. Judging from the hardened earth and rubble, this course had most likely been a riverbed at one time. Most of the villagers lived in caves in the hills, but there was also a *mandy* of traders here and we were able to replenish our provisions. Walking some distance farther, we passed through the hamlet known as Maakram. Another three miles brought us to Pala. Since the sun was setting by the time we reached Pala, we camped there.

Lippu Pass: On Indian Soil Once More

29 July. The day's journey started with an extremely steep climb over a number of small hills. Rivulets of melted snow ran along the path. The climb became even more difficult as we proceeded.

Nevertheless, the scenery was enthralling, and the sight of snow-covered peaks gently breaking through the soft cloud cover kept our spirits high. The blue clouds tumbling across the hills reminded us of the sweet baby Krishna at play. The steepness of the slope made climbing especially difficult for the mules, so we dismounted. Using our staffs and taking each step with utmost care, we advanced on foot–eventually reaching the summit of Lippu Pass.

This summit lies at an elevation of 16,800 feet. If you look in one direction, the glare of the white snow is literally blinding. Looking in the opposite direction, the eyes are soothed by the pale green waters of Lippu Lake. The sight of the river Kali, flowing down from the lake with a gentle murmur, is equally refreshing. Sometimes Mother Nature presents the most terrifying appearance; at other times she wears the sweetest, tenderest smile.

India lies to the south of Lippu Pass. We looked forward to stepping onto her soil once again after an absence of 22 days. Still, the descent went very slowly due to the thick snow and thin air. Large chunks of ice from the glaciers slid down into valleys that were so deep they seemed to be bottomless. Our feet sank wherever the snow had melted on the path. When we finally stepped onto the soil of Bharat, we temporarily forgot all of these dangers in the midst of our joy at being in India once more. Swami Premanandaji, who had gone on ahead, now welcomed us at a tea kiosk with something to eat. Since leaving Milam on the way up, we had only been able to get bread, potatoes, pickle and dried vegetables. From here on, there would be places where we could buy fresh vegetables.

We rested at the tea kiosk until 1:00 in the afternoon, and then walked on to Kaalaapaani. This spot is 12,000 feet high. Since there were no houses or huts in which to rest here, we pitched our tent. Kaalaapaani means "black water" and is named for the dark, muddy spring found nearby. Here we met three renunciates on their way to Kailash who were overjoyed at the opportunity to hear of our experiences and learn what was ahead. We told them what food and medicines they were likely to need, and were glad to pass on to them those items from our supply of drugs, food and clothing that we no longer needed. That night we slept in the tent for the last time.

A Close Call

30 July. We left Kaalaapaani and walked a long distance along the river bank. The path was rugged, but not steep. It followed the banks of the Kali for many miles, crossing the river by a narrow bridge where she turned. We walked farther still and came upon another narrow river, flowing under a narrow bridge. Some of our group had already crossed by the time I reached the river. I, too, started to cross the bridge, but when I got to the middle I saw a goat with packs on its back starting toward me from the opposite shore. Since the bridge was far to narrow to allow for passing, it was obvious that either the goat or the pilgrim would have to turn back immediately. Otherwise, one of them would soon be floating in the river. Consequently, I quickly returned the way I had come.

The goat continued coming toward me. I walked faster and faster until I was safely back on the shore. The goat, however, was also anxious to get ashore, and jumped from the bridge when there were still five or six feet to go. The next thing I knew the animal was struggling for its life in the rapids; can anyone change the course of fate? I prayed to the Lord and stood repeating the *maha mrityunjaya mantra*. As the goat slowly drifted closer to the shore, its owner—who had been on the opposite bank—came running across the bridge. He was pleased to discover that the animal was still alive, and when it had come within reach, he pulled it out of the water. I was also relieved, and happily started across the bridge again. The owner of the goat, however, must have blamed me for the fall, because he angrily pelted a stone at me. By God's grace it missed its mark, but it came very, very close.

Facing Death Again

As the afternoon wore on, the river passed far behind us and my legs started to ache with fatigue. Soon they were begging me to let them rest. When a free mule came by, I mounted it. A heavy rain suddenly started to fall, and I opened my umbrella. The mule was walking slowly beneath some trees. When I closed the umbrella to duck under a low branch, the animal became alarmed and jumped ahead. I fell face down on a rock and called out "*Hari OM*." My breathing stopped and I could feel the life rapidly departing from my body. I knew that I faced death, but the Lord apparently had other plans for me: a voice within me whispered, "Breathe in. Hard!" With all the strength I could muster, I managed to breathe in once, then again. Slowly, I was able to breathe the life back into this frame. I was still stunned from the impact of the fall, however, and continued to lie motionless on the rock.

When I opened my eyes again, I saw the mule drivers standing around me administering first aid. Their eyes were filled with concern. The right side of my chest and both knees had severe concussions. Since I was unable to stand, all those present together lifted me onto the back of a mule. The driver led the animal. The pain in my chest increased with each faltering step of the mule as it descended the slope. Still, the desire to have the experience of the divine again was so great that I would have gladly risked my life over and over to get it.

Garbiang: Last Border Stop

The scenery along the path started to change but still held equally-great attraction. The mountains reached high into the skies, roses bloomed in varied colors, pine trees clustered in forests, rivers and brooks babbled amidst them all. One brook wound its way this way and that, divided and then magically disappeared directly into the side of a hill. The water that splashed near the bank bathed the passerby with pearl-like drops. This balm of nature was so soothing that I had almost forgotten the pain of the body when we reached Garbiang around three in the afternoon.

Garbiang, at 14,300 feet, is the last village on the Indian border. The river Kali flows nearby, but since its course lies deep within a valley, there is little fresh water available to the people here. Still, Garbiang is an important center for the many traders from Bhutan. The last Indian post office on this route is also here. I collected the many letters that had been awaiting me. The aches in the rest of my body kept company with the ache in my chest. I asked for a bed to be prepared and leaned back on it. With one hand I pressed down on my chest. Its condition had not improved despite applications of heated saffron and *ghee*. Mr. Ramdas sat by my side and opened my letters for me while I read through them. Only then did I fully realize why the life that had already departed from this body had also returned to live in it again.

The Hearts of Devotees

The prayers of devotees for our safe return had empowered us to accomplish this pilgrimage. Many had performed *japa* (repetition of the Lord's name) on our behalf. Others had joined in the *akanda nama bhajan*. Still others had held fast to the feet of the Lord of Kailash in their hearts, composing songs of praise to Him daily. This loving devotion was also expressed in their many letters. I spent the rest of the day lying in bed and joined the evening *bhajan* from there. The following day was 31 July. The drivers of the mules wanted to return to their village from here. We were sincerely grateful to them and happily paid their wages, giving them whatever clothing and other articles we could spare as well. They bade us an affectionate farewell and took leave.

The path down from here is very difficult for mules, so we engaged porters instead. We left Garbiang by 12:00 noon. The day before I had received a blow taking me to the very brink of death. Now, with no mules to ride, I had to proceed on foot. Though I suspected that I might have fractured a rib, nothing could be done about it here. I decided that I would consult my friend, Dr. Krishnan, when we reached Bombay. As I started walking, I was very grateful to find that Mr. Ramdas, who normally went ahead with some of the others, now stayed back to keep me company—as he continued to do from that day on. I praised the Lord for granting me such mercies whenever I had need of them. What could I do in return for all of the devotees, friends and well-wishers who rescued me from the very gates of death by their prayers and *japa,* enabling me to continue serving the Lord and His children? I could only pray that He shower them all with His blessings of health and happiness.

Top: Cave dwelling carved out of the rock. The small black holes are the entrances.
Below: Up and down, the path is always rugged.

Top: Just a valley for the pilgrims to pass through.
Below: Premanandaji and Praveen in front of the sleeping and kitchen tents.

Chapter 19
The Final Phase of the Walk

On our way up to the holy Kailash, we had started walking at Bhageswaram, proceeding through Siyamathara, Ramganga, Quintee, Girham, Kalamuni, Pethuli, Rethi, Gowri Ganga, Baldi Ganga, Rupshibagar, Nehar and Martholi to the Indian border town of Milam.

In returning from Kailash, we would set out from the border town of Garbiang and continue on through Bukti, Maalpa, Jipthi, Sardhaan, Pangu, Yela, Dharchula, Askot, Dhal and Bijapur back to Bhageswaram.

Bukti is a village five miles from Garbiang. The first two miles were a gradual climb, the other three a steep descent. A dark green forest stands like the long wall of a fortress along the route; tall hills rise up ahead like towers. The distant snow-covered peaks shine like the crowns of temples under the golden rays of the sun. The valleys that wind their way here and there form moats around the village.

Bukti stands in the midst of all this like a castle where Mother Nature has taken abode. Rock slides are common here during heavy rains. In many places, it behooves the pilgrim to walk quickly and listen carefully for the sound of stones rolling down from the peaks. If he does not take shelter in the slopes of the hill quickly, a rolling stone might take him along for company on its way down to the river Kali. Bukti has a small school, where most of the pilgrims breaking journey here find shelter for the night. We took shelter there, too.

Maalpa: Using Hands To Climb

1 August. Maalpa is seven miles from Bukti. This village is enriched by the waters or the river Maalpa from which it takes its name. There are no permanent residents in Maalpa, but there is a

small pilgrims' rest with two rooms. The walls and roof of the rest are slates of stone; the floor is uneven, and one has to level it with leaves and shrubs before spreading out his bedding. This rest is near the house of the postman and the cottages of the road menders.

Maalpa, surrounded by hills of rock, is another natural fortress. Two rivers, the Maalpa and the Kali, run at opposite ends of the village. Their noise is deafening. The soil here is enriched by the waters of these rivers and abounds with a lush growth of trees, shrubs and vines. The route from Bukti to Maalpa is filled with danger. On one side of the path, steep hills rise to a height of 5,000 feet; on the other side is a steep drop to the narrow valley where the river Kali runs far below. It is almost impossible to manage the descent without the aid of a spiked staff.

At some spots we had to hold on to the low-growing shrubs and vines while climbing; at others we had to get down on our knees and crawl. Unfortunately, this method of ascent does not offer much opportunity to appreciate the beauty of nature. In the spring, one often comes across Tibetans who are returning to Tibet with their herds of goats after spending the winter here. If one does not quickly find a spot in the slopes to get off the path and make way for the oncoming herds, he should be ready to sacrifice himself to the Kali Ganga.

Jipthi: A Frugal Place

Walking about 18 miles along various river banks, we passed through Maalpa and on to Bindu, a mile-long fort lying between two huge rocks. On the steeper slopes, we had to sit on the ground and use both hands and feet to work our way down. The paths on opposite sides of the rivers were connected by narrow logs; crossing these makeshift bridges makes you dizzy. In some places, we had to jump out of the way when stones rattled down from the peaks overhead; in others, the slippery rocks beneath our feet could easily have made us fall. We were graced to make our way past all of these obstacles, however, and eventually reached the village of Jipthi.

Jipthi means "frugal;" it lies at a height of 8,000 feet and is very aptly named. The village is compact, and the path is very narrow here. We found only one structure in Jipthi, and that was a tea kiosk. Sri Sathur Singh, the owner of the kiosk, received us kindly. Fresh fruit is available here off and on, and we were very happy to find apples and bananas served with the tea. A lovely flower called *dolia* is the one abundant thing in Jipthi.

Sardhaan Path: All Ups and Downs

2 August. Walking about a mile from Jipthi through Sardaali Sardhaan, we reached the bank of the Sangula River. On the other side of the river, we entered a thick forest. The entire path was muddy and slippery from the frequent rains in this area. Three miles were a continuous uphill climb from which we then had to climb down. Another upward climb followed. The path continued in this way until we reached Sardhaan. Here Sri Malhotra, the head of the woolen apparel weaving center, welcomed us warmly and invited us to spend the night in his home. Unfortunately, there was not time to visit the Sri Narayan Ashram, which we learned was only a few miles away.

Pangu: Some Unique Trees

3 August. Next we came to Pangu. This village is a part of Bhutan and lies at a height of 7,000 feet. The Dawala Ganga forms its northern boundary. Though trade is the main occupation of the inhabitants, many of them wear the sacred thread of the Brahmins (the priestly caste) of India. The Bhutanis have both trade and marriage relations with the Tibetans. They resemble the Chinese in facial structure and speak a dialect that is a mixture of Hindi and Tibetan.

As we descended to Pangu, we passed a great many trees with colorful pieces of cloth hanging from the branches like multicolored fruit. From a distance, these appeared to be cloth-bearing trees, and the appearance was quite convincing. Of course, we knew this could not be so; when we reached Pangu, we learned that the cloths were actually prayer flags hung in the trees by devotees in worship of the Lord.

We rested that noon at the residence of a relative of Swami Bagawathanandaji, and enjoyed a spirited *bhajan* there. After a lunch of many appetizing courses, we resumed our walk. It was now two in the afternoon.

Yela: Beauty and Danger

Yela abounds with *kela*. In Hindi, *kela* means bananas. This village is very sparsely populated, with only a few houses spread far apart. The shopkeepers here are very genial, though, and gladly provide travelers with shelter. Bananas and *ghee* are available in abundance, although water–in spite of frequent rainfalls–is dear in some parts of the region.

The path followed along the course of Kali Ganga, thrilling the pilgrim with grand waterfalls. It became narrower from Yela on. The first three miles wound down the slopes and had to be descended with extreme care. Next, there was a stretch of sandy slopes and rugged ups and downs, which posed a danger of its own. Topping even this was an area we soon came to where the slope of the hill was almost perpendicular.

Danger from Stones

Since stones on this stretch are continually rolling out from underfoot, it is difficult for mules to carry baggage. However, some courageous individuals do at times attempt to lead animals with packs here. It was near Yela that I slipped and fell on a rock while walking along a river bank. Glad to be escaping with a minor injury, I cheerily continued. Before we reached Dharchula however, I was hit on the arm by a stone that came tumbling down the mountainside. This blow gave me some pain. I mused on my fourth encounter with stone on this trip. Resolving that all the dangers in life are to be faced, I boldly continued on my way.

A Hair-Raising Spectacle

At the banks of the Kali Ganga, I saw a hair-raising sight that filled me with fear and amazement. The rough waters of the river cascaded down the steep hills with great force. Nevertheless, a rope was tied across the river, with a triangular frame hanging from it. A man was dangling over the water, his legs in the frame and both hands holding the rope. Another, thinner rope was tied around the middle of the frame, the ends of which were held by a man on each bank who pulled the frame and its occupant across the river. As we watched, we wondered whether this daring soul was crossing the River Kali...or the river of death. The courage of the hill tribes has no match.

Dharchula: God's Grace

We proceeded from here, soon arriving in Dharchula. This large city is an important trade center for the Bhutanis. Four towering hills border the four sides of the city. Food crops–such as wheat, mango, citrus and banana–abound here. Travelers can easily find accommodations in the many *dak* bungalows and charitable rests found in this area.

Around 11 in the morning, we went to bathe in the river on the outskirts of the town. On the way, I saw another "hair-raising spectacle": Dr. Krishnan of Bombay, who was on his way to Kailash with a group of pilgrims. This totally unexpected meeting overwhelmed me. Who could have fulfilled my need to consult the doctor, which I had intended to do days later upon reaching Bombay, but the Lord of creation Himself? In ordinary circumstances, it is not always easy to see the Lord at work but, in a case such as this, the works of His hand are clearly evident. Had not my soul and body become His the day I surrendered to Him? Then surely He was taking care of them. I offered Him my grateful prayers. While speaking with Dr. Krishnan and his group about the pilgrimage, I told him about my chest injury. An immediate examination showed that there was no serious damage. The doctor advised me what to do and offered his prayers to God. I thanked him, and we continued on our separate ways. Here is matter for thought for those who do not believe in the grace of God.

Fort Palawa

5 August. Five porters requested to be paid off, and our departure was delayed a few hours while we hired new ones. The road here was motorable, and walking was easy. When we reached Kalima, we rested for awhile before going on to Fort Palawa. The fort lies in a valley on the banks of Kali Ganga, 11 miles from Dharchula. We found that there were no permanent residents here either. The Bhutanis come down to Palawa during the winter and return to the hills higher up in the spring.

We left Fort Palawa at 6:00 in the morning on the 6th of August and followed the course of the Kali Ganga once more. Eventually the

Kali Ganga merges into the Gowri Ganga; the union of these two powerful and holy rivers is a thrilling sight. The village found at this spot is known as Jalaji. At Jalaji, we found an ashram and a beautiful Siva temple surrounded by a flower garden. About a mile from here, we crossed the Gowri Ganga by a swing bridge. The next three and a half miles were a steady climb, and we did not reach Askot until 2:30 in the afternoon.

Askot: Crossing the Jungle

Askot is about twelve miles from Fort Palawa. Here we found a *dak* bungalow, a post office and a few shops owned by Bhutanis. We stayed in the public works department circuit bungalow, situated in the center of a hill that was constantly enveloped by snow-white clouds. A majestic and colorful painting of the palace of a one-time ruler decorated the bungalow. Leaving the town of Askot on the morning of the seventh, we continued to Narayan Nagar. This is a place that arose out of the divine service of Swami Narayanji Maharaj. The Babu Maha Vidyalayam (high school) founded by Swamiji is the most important structure here. At the time of our visit, however, the school was closed for the holidays. After looking around Narayan Nagar, we walked a distance of nine miles, crossing the village Didihut, and entered the jungle.

We had five miles to cross through the thick jungle. Even the rays of the sun could not fully penetrate the dense growth; they only peeped through here and there at scattered intervals. The ever-present possibility of attack by wild animals caused us some concern. Brushing aside physical fatigue and the pleading of our legs, we walked at a fast pace without stopping–until we realized that we were lost. Just then a hill tribesman miraculously appeared–surely sent by the Lord–to feed us with curd and take us back to the right path. When we arrived in Dhal at last, our legs, which carried us 18 miles that day, were given a much-deserved rest.

Bhageswaram Again

8 August. The porters who had come from Garbiang declined to go any farther this morning. Our journey was resumed after once more engaging new men and mules. The path cut across Sakodi

A hair-raising spectacle. Crossing the rushing river in a triangle of thin slats of wood suspended on a rope high above the current. Aides on the two banks are pulling the occupant across with ropes attached to the frame. Is he crossing a jungle stream, or the river of death?

and Kumodi villages. (The bus service ordinarily serving this route had been temporarily suspended for the rainy season.) The ground between the villages was covered with thick jungle brush, but our feet seemed to find their own way along the dark, overgrown path. When we reached the outskirts of the village Bijapur, it was well after sundown and pitch dark.

Only a distance of a mile separated us from the village. At that late hour, to our great surprise, a truck came up behind us. Its arrival seemed to be a gift from Mother Kumodi to relieve the suffering of her children. The driver stopped and picked us up, driving us straight to Bhageswaram. We arrived at last at ten o'clock that night. The mules and baggage arrived around three o'clock the following afternoon.

The End of the Kailash Pilgrimage

The pilgrimage on foot which had started on the 8th of June 1958 ended exactly two months later on the 8th of August.

We spent the whole of the following day resting at Bhageswaram and left for Kathkodam by bus on the 10th. Divan Singh, our capable cook and constant companion, took leave of us as we boarded. Our hearts were overflowing with affection and gratitude; we supplemented his wages with some of our own possessions and wished him farewell.

The bus trip was soon halted by a tree that had fallen across the road in the heavy rain. It was a long time before the road was cleared for the bus, and when we finally reached Kathkodam, we spent the rest of the night in the railway station.

Since our train was not leaving until 3:45 the following afternoon, we decided to visit the beautiful summer resort of Nainital. A state taxi took us there. It was a delightful morning, spent boating on the lake. We enjoyed the colourful environment, but returned to the Kathkodam railway station in time to have lunch before boarding the afternoon train. We slept on the train that night, lost to the world. The holy city of Mathura greeted us at dawn. There, with reluctant heart, I bade farewell to Swami Premanandaji, Sri Praveen Nanawathi, Ramdasji and Swami Bagawathanandaji—my constant companion of the pilgrimage—to board the Grand Trunk Express for Delhi.

We had walked a distance of 800 miles during the pilgrimage. We had ascended to an altitude of 19,000 feet. It would be childish to claim that we had achieved these feats ourselves. The absolute truth is that His grace, guarding us every moment from within and from without, from left and from right, from ahead and behind and from above and below–together with the prayers of our loving devotees– had led us there and had guided us back again.

Who could reach Kailash without His Grace?

Top left: Kurukshethra, where Lord Krishna imparted the holy *Bhagavad Gita* to Arjuna.
Top right: Kulu Valley girls.
Below: Sri Nagar: the temple of Lord Siva.

Chapter 20
Amarnath

Amarnath, the Lord of Kashmir, who had seen me showered with the blessings of Lord Siva of Kailash, decided to shower me in His grace, too. During our stay at the Bhageswaram rest house, while conversing with my fellow pilgrims about the wonderful divine game the Lord plays with us, I once again felt the call of the Supreme Lord, Parameswara–and immediately resolved to visit His holy abode at Amarnath.

In order to enter the state of Kashmir, it is necessary to have an entry permit from the Indian Ministry of Defense. I obtained the required permit, as well as any additional items I would be needing for the pilgrimage, during a four-day stopover in Delhi. By the 16th of August I was ready to leave for Patankot by the express train. Kurukshetra lies along this route, so I had the good fortune to be able to visit that greatly revered place where Sri Krishna imparted the teaching of the holy *Bhagavad Gita* to Arjuna. A little farther along is the world-famous Bhakra Nangal Dam, which I also visited. From here I continued through the Kulu Valley to Manaali, another place of world-renowned beauty, and on to Patankot. The temple of Vashista Maharishi and a warm water tank lie nearby. I bathed in the tank and offered my prayers in the temple of Vashista before boarding the express bus to Sri Nagar. Entry permits were checked along the way.

Jammu, Kashmir: The Gates of Heaven

The bus to Sri Nagar left at noon and reached Jammu by evening. Jammu, 67 miles from Patankot, is the winter capital of Kashmir. I offered my prayers at the famous Ragunath Temple and other holy shrines there that night, and resumed my bus journey the next morning. The entire countryside was a vision of beauty. Literally millions of flowers in full bloom filled the air with their perfume. Golden wheat fields and colorful orchards actually competed with the flowers in beauty. The apples grown here were a special delight, too, each one tasting sweeter than the last.

We soon came to Panigal Pass, and a long tunnel. The elevation at this point was 9,000 feet. I got off the bus, thinking that it might be nice to walk through the tunnel. Coming out of the other end was like walking into a dream. The gates of heaven stood open before me, revealing a scene of astounding beauty. Kashmir spreads over an area of 80 miles in length and 25 miles in breadth. The entire area is fortified by high peaks and crowned with snow. Turning my head in any direction brought an equally spectacular view. As I looked, I wondered whether God had created all this scenery to delight the eyes . . . or the eyes to appreciate the scenery! The simple answer came to me at once. One is not for the other. Both are for Him. All of creation is His person. All acts are His acts. I remained immersed in such thoughts for some time. Finally I heard a voice saying, "Swamiji, were you intending to stay behind here?" Turning, I saw the bus conductor standing beside me, awaiting my reply. Only then did I come back to earth and hasten to board the bus, grateful that he had not left me behind.

Sri Nagar

The whole day was spent traveling by bus. By dusk we had covered the 200 miles to Sri Nagar and reached the pilgrims' rest run by the state there. An entire chapter could be written in praise of that pilgrims' rest. Everything that could possibly be thought of for the comfort of the pilgrim had been provided. Sri Nagar is the summer capital of Kashmir. The crowning glory of this city is the Sankaracharya Hill. On the summit of the hill is a temple dedicated to Lord Siva. There the Lord appears in the holy form of the Siva *Lingam*. This is the largest Siva *Lingam* to be found anywhere in the world. I stood on the hilltop and looked down. All of Sri Nagar lay before me, adorned with bungalows of many different colors. River boats, house boats, swans, lotuses in full bloom and tender vines–all draped in the beautiful costume of the Holy Mother–lay sprinkled across the countryside. The children of the Lord also appeared in holy costume–in their various colors, shapes and sizes–walking their many holy paths through this wonderland to realize His presence in all.

Here in Kashmir, the Lord Amarnath has taken abode in a cave at an elevation of 14,000 feet. Within the cave He can be seen in the holy form of a dazzling *Siva Lingam* of pure white snow. This form only appears for a few days each year during the time of the full moon in the Tamil month of *Aavani*. The full moon day itself is the day especially set aside to worship at His feet. I started out on the 25th of August–four days ahead of this important date–in order to make the pilgrimage at this most auspicious time. I spent that night at Pahalgam (7,500 feet) and the following day made the necessary arrangements to complete the pilgrimage on foot.

Everything for the Pilgrims' Convenience

It is only 32 miles from Pahalgam to Amarnath cave, but there are many pilgrims' rests operated by the Kashmir government along the way. First aid camps and other facilities are set up at places where overnight stops are made. Still the number of pilgrims who come at this particular time is so great that many of them prefer the convenience of hiring mules and porters and transporting their own camping equipment, tents, food and provisions. Mules are often hired for riding as well. The fees for tents, mules and porters are fixed by the state, and state officials make all of the arrangements.

On my journey to Kailash I had been happy to share a tent with others; now I thought I would like to have a little solitude, so I rented a small tent for myself. I brought just enough food–some biscuits, bread and butter–to sustain me for the duration. I also kept clothes and bedding to a minimum, thinking that if I had been able to tame the cold of Kailash, I could now think lightly of the cold of Amarnath. The overall weight came to about 25 kilograms or 55 pounds, which could easily be carried by a single porter.

In August 1958 there were approximately 5,000 devotees, 4,000 porters and 3,000 mules making this pilgrimage. These figures are based on the statistics maintained by the state. The head of the Kashmiri *madam* is in charge of the pilgrimage; until he leaves on the path with the *Chadi*–the holy emblem of the celebration–no one is allowed to move even a single step.

Top: The holy *Chadi* under an umbrella tent.
Below: Self-portrait taken by the author at the top of the hardest climb on the way
to Amarnath.

The Holy Emblem

In the days of yore, a group of devotees prayed in this spot to Birungi Maharishi that he might show them the way to attain salvation; the sage blessed them with the reply that they should go to Amarnath, pray to the Lord there and thus obtain their desire. The happy group of devotees proceeded to Amamath to have the *darshan* of the Lord. On the way they were accosted by *rakshasas*–giant demons–and ran back to the Maharishi full of fear. Birungi Maharishi told them: "Fear not! Pray to Dhakshaka, the king of the serpents. He will bless you with Lord Parameswara's staff. If you carry this in your hand, the *rakshasas* will retreat in fear." The devotees did as they were told and with the *Sivathandam*–the mace of Siva–completed the pilgrimage successfully. It is this holy mace, called *Chadi,* that is taken ahead by the head of the *madam,* and which the pilgrims follow.

The Start

26 August. The air rang out with voices calling, "Victory to the Lord of Amarnath! Bolo Amarnathki Jai!" The *Chadi* was taken down the path, and the pilgrims started along behind. Twelve thousand lives filed closely by on the narrow route, carefully avoiding the deathtraps in search of the feet of their Lord. Proceeding at a very slow pace, we covered nine miles and reached Chandanwari at 9,500 feet about noon.

Here we found that a delightful townlet of tents, temporary trade stalls, and other such sights, had sprung up for the occasion. I pitched my tent at a suitable spot and gave the porter some money to buy his lunch. After eating some of my biscuits, I rested for a while. Later, I meditated and passed a peaceful night in my tent.

27 August, Morning. By the time I finished packing, the porters and mules were already advancing with their loads of baggage. Within just a few minutes after dawn, the entire tent city had vanished. Around one and a half miles from Chandanwari, we came to Pissugatti. Here the slope was so steep that we had a great deal of difficulty trying to climb without injuring our knees. Silence reigned on the tortuous upward climbs, but on the flat stretches and descents it was broken by the sound of voices chanting, "Victory to the Lord!" Is it not true that we remember the Lord constantly in times of trouble, and rarely

144

Screaming Mikes

Once again, the fatigue of the climb was soothed by the sights of nature that came into view from the summit. White snow-covered peaks and green forests stood in beautiful contrast on either side. From the top of the hill we could see the path leading down through a deep abyss. Just looking at it made us feel giddy. Yet, with steadfast faith in the certainty that the Lord of Amarnath would bring us safely to His feet, we proceeded. On the way to Vaavjaan–a distance of eight miles– we passed the lake of Seshnag, which was covered with a blanket of glistening snow. Along the way, the microphones of the state aid group began to scream, "Hariharan of Allahabad is wanted by his companion Gulab Singh. . . Ramdas and brother from Ramnagar are anxious about the missing Sita. . . Mannarsamy of Madhya Pradesh is looking for the whereabouts of his mule and baggage. . . Six-year old Pushpa is crying for her mother. . . Those concerned please call at the camp of the aid group."

Such appeals continuously rang through the air. When thousands of devotees assemble, it is always common for many of them to lose their belongings or get separated from their party. The first aid groups here are not second in their service. Their assistance to the pilgrims is inestimable, and has saved many, many lives.

The next day we were on our way to Mahagunas–a pass at a height of 14,700 feet–when we saw a tea kiosk. This came as a great surprise to us, since we knew there was not water to be found for miles around. We soon learned that the tea was made by melting some of the snow that had piled up on the roof of the tent. We had some of this tea and descended to a height of 13,000 feet to camp at Panchatharani.

Holy Full Moon Day

The next day, 29 August, was the holy full moon day. At 3:30 in the morning I left for Amarnath Cave, leaving my belongings and tent in the care of the porter. It was cold and dark. The entire path was covered with granular snow. Only by the mercy and grace of the Lord was I able to get there safely. I could have reached the cave by 7:00 a.m., but the time slipped by as I became absorbed in the joy of serving His devotees along the way.

Many pilgrims slipped on the ice along the hazardous five-mile path. Those who were old and feeble soon grew numb with cold and frequently fell into the snow. Some of the children cried to their mothers that they were cold; others just cried, not even knowing the reason why. I served the Lord as best I could by assisting the suffering ones and reached the cave at last at about 10:00 in the morning.

The cave itself lies at a height of 14,000 feet. It is 55 feet across, 50 feet long and 45 feet high. I bathed near the cave in the Amarawathi spring, whose waters come from melting snow. With an offering of flowers in my hands and an offering of love in my heart, I entered the cave. My entire body tingled with the thrill. My heart was exuberant with joy. Here I beheld the holy person of the Lord of Amarnath. I clasped my hands and prayed. I fell at His feet in worship. I arose and stood reverently in His presence, wondering at the grace He bestows on His devotees by appearing before them as the *Lingam*. It is His gift of grace to allow them this experience of seeing His holy person. The form soon melts away, but the realization of his presence remains with the devotee for all of time.

A *puja* was performed. Two white birds flew into the cave; this was considered to be a sign that the Lord was pleased with the offering and had accepted the *puja*. Having received the wealth of His blessings, I paid reverence to Him once more and started the return journey. Just to the left of the cave's opening is a pit of holy ash. This ash is a gift of nature, and the amount in the pit never diminishes no matter how much is taken from it. I, too, received some of this *prasad* and started off.

The Return

Reluctantly, I retraced my steps to Panchatharani. After relaxing there awhile, I folded up the tent and continued the five miles to Vaavjaan with the other returning pilgrims. We spent the night at Vaavjaan, resuming our trek in the morning. There had been a hailstorm farther along, and when we reached the point where the storm had been, the path became dangerously slippery. Walking very cautiously—and holding on to each other for support—we passed through Chandanwari and finally reached Pahalgam. Thus, the pilgrimage to holy Amarnath, a five-day journey of 64 miles made on foot, was brought to completion. It was the 30th of August. The

Top: Seshnag: a beautiful pond on the way to Amarnath.
Below: The five miles from Panchatharani is a path covered with snow.

Top: A line of pilgrims in a snow valley. What a price to pay in order to see God.
Below: At last we are in the Holy Amarnath Cave. It is huge: 50 feet by 50 feet by 50 feet.

following morning the bus took me through Anandanaag, Kannapal, Achabal, Gogarnaag, Sangam and Avandipur to deposit me at Sri Nagar, where I engaged a houseboat for a few days. Plenty of natural springs and other scenic beauty abound in Kashmir, and I decided to take a little time to travel into various parts of this region.

On the 5th of September, I finally left for Patankot via Jammu by special state bus. At Patankot I boarded the bus for Amritsar, arriving there that same evening. A very special Golden Temple of the Sikh faith is found at Amritsar, as well as the famous Jalianwala Gardens. I had the privilege of visiting these places, as well as some of the many silk-weaving factories located in the area.

Top: The author and his host, Sri Panna Lal, visit the Golden Temple at Amritsar.
Below: The houseboat that served as my home.
Opposite page, top: Achabal spring, Kashmir.
Opposite page, below: The beautiful little taxi boats.

150

Sivananda *Jayanthi*

Leaving by train the next night, I reached Sivananda Nagar at Rishikesh on the auspicious day of 8 September 1958, the holy 72nd *Jayanthi* (birthday) of my revered master Jagadguru Sri Swami Sivananda Saraswati. There I joined the thousands of devotees who had gathered to worship at the feet of their holy Master and to bathe in the ocean of his divine love.

I had the privilege of narrating in his presence the experiences of the holy pilgrimage to Kailash that had been accomplished through his blessings. I mentally dedicated all of the benefits of my pilgrimage at his golden feet. I was immersed in endless joy.

Throughout the day large crowds assembled at Sivananda Nagar to sing his praise and worship at his holy feet. Devotees from every part of the globe had gathered there. They were all members of the one Sivananda family who had come together, breaking the chains of caste, creed, religion, country, color, race and language. Was it not one of the great lessons of the pilgrimage that all these names and forms are His children, dressed in His holy costume? No doubt, once that divine Light of Truth is realized, all of these are seen as but reflections of that one Light.

There was a grand *pada puja* to the holy Master. Offerings were showered before him. A *maharani*, in keeping with her status, heaped fruits, vegetables, clothing and more at his feet. Those who were poor in worldly wealth but rich in devotion made their simple and humble offerings. The holy Master's eyes of love looked on each one with equal affection; what attracted him was not external things, but the heart of purity and love he saw within. There was no difference in his look of grace from one to another as it fell in turn on each sincere devotee. The thousands assembled there were also served with food. Cultural events, such as folk dance, music, *bhajans*, films and more followed in the afternoon and continued until dawn.

The following day also witnessed many events. Throughout these activities, the devotees gradually began to get ready to go home. They slowly filed before the holy Master in small groups to receive his blessings before departure. I, too, now prepared to leave, and waited for an opportunity to speak with him alone. After receiving more advice about the ways and means of bringing his message of Divine Life to the many sincere seekers in Sri Lanka, I prostrated at his holy feet and took leave. That same night I boarded the train to Delhi.

From Delhi I returned to Sri Lanka via Bombay, Madras, Coimbatore and Thiruchirappali, arriving on the 29th of September. Large groups had assembled to receive me at the airport in Kankesanthurai and Ratmalana. I was immersed in the joy of sharing the holy *prasad of* the Lord with His loving children. Today, I am still sharing that great *prasad*–and that great joy–with one and all. It is my sincere wish and prayer that the whole world should experience this endless happiness.

Victory to the Supreme Lord! May His grace be unto all! May the entire creation be filled with peace and joy! *OM Shanti, Shanti, Shanti.*

With Satgurudev Sivanandaji Maharaj on the auspicious occasion of his holy *Jayanthi*, 8 September 1958.

Appendix

Forewords
(As they appeared in the original edition)

I was one of those who were blessed with the privilege of seeing Swami Satchidananda off at Colombo Airport as he left for Kailash. My heart was filled with longing. I, too, desired to go, but in order to see Kailash in this form, does not the Lord's blessing have to be there as well as the desire?

As Swamiji left with the full blessings of the Lord, my prayer was that he would remember me while he was there. He did not forget. He wrote me from various stops along the way, and when he returned, he gave me a stone which he had brought all the way back from Kailash for me. It blesses me and reminds me always of his great love.

My opinion is that Swamiji did not undertake this pilgrimage for his personal benefit. This book proves beyond a doubt that his journey was for our sake. In recounting the story, step by step, Swamiji takes us along with him to Kailash. This is not a book about pilgrimage, but a pilgrimage in itself, and all those who read it can climb in his footsteps to the very summit of human experience. It is a privilege to be cherished.

We are forever indebted to Swamiji for traveling to Kailash, irrespective of the difficulties, and for enabling us to share his remarkable experiences. Even more important, we are indebted to him for enabling us to know that supreme joy of seeing God.

Colombo
Sri Lanka   K. P. HARAN

One of the fields in which Tamil literature needs to be enriched is that of travel. There are many fascinating books in Western languages that transport readers to the farthest reaches of the globe, but this field has not yet been sufficiently explored in the Tamil language.

Kailash Journal is not only an excellent spiritual book to the pious, but a thrilling travelogue to one and all. It includes vivid descriptions of not only the geography, but the scenery, climate and people of the Himalayan region, with guided tours of monasteries and temples as well. As such, this book has great social and historical interest, in addition to its deep and perceptive spirituality.

Upon his return from pilgrimage to Mount Kailash, the revolutionary monk, Sri Swami Satchidanandaji Maharaj, wrote these reports on his travels for the weekly journal *Sunthanthiran.* They were serialized over the course of half a year. Each piece was enormously popular, and all of them have now been put together to tell the whole story from start to finish.

Already known as a good orator, Swamiji Maharaj has now established himself as an equally-excellent author. We are all blessed to have this opportunity to benefit from his journey and his journal.

May his holy name live long. May his holy service ever expand.

Colombo
Sri Lanka

S. T. SIVANAYAGAM
Editor, *Sunthanthiran*

154

The abode of Lord Siva on the silvery peak of Mount Kailash in the holy Himalayas is full of natural beauty and scenic grandeur. Here the great Lord has performed many a miracle.

There are thousands of caves in the Himalayas, where great sages live meditating on the Lord. The gentle and soft music of water flowing over the hills seems to repeat the syllable "OM," resounding as sweet and clear as if it were coming out of a silver *veena*. There you see a sea of snow covering the Himalayan peaks. Flowers of different hues and trees of different shades, butterflies and birds humming around, are all sights to be seen in the great Himalayas.

Long and weary forests with tall and towering trees, high and steep mountain slopes, ferocious animals, rapid and dangerous rivers, chill and biting cold winds, severe storms, rolling rocks, shivering snow and suspended bridges that dance in the wind are among the many perils that abound in the high Himalayas.

The author of this wonderful book, Sri Swami Satchidanandaji Maharaj, visited the formidable Mount Kailash in his own mortal body. It is perhaps one of those miracles of the Lord that he came back to narrate his experience in sweet and humble words, and to share his adventure and his joy with us.

With divine ecstasy and tears of joy, he feasted on the glory of the Lord. And with His grace, he has given us all a taste of the nectar he drank there. He has captured our longing hearts and shown us the way to the abode of the Lord. May he live long and well, ever in His service. He is a great and pure soul, indeed.

Navalappati   PARAMAHAMSADHASAN
Sri Lanka

Glossary

A

aalayam: a temple

abhayam: fearlessness

abhaya mudra: a gesture indicating there is no need to fear

akanda nama bhajan: continuous chanting of the name of God

asura: a demon

B

Bhagavad Gita: the Hindu scripture in which Lord Krishna instructs His disciple Arjuna

bhajan: a song or prayer in praise of the Lord

brahmachari: one practicing celibacy, either in the student stage of life or as a monk

C

Chadi: the mace of Lord Siva; the holy emblem that leads the procession in pilgrimage to Amarnath (see page 142)

chaitanyam: the all-pervading consciousness that feels and understands (see page 92)

chapathi: a type of Indian flatbread made from wheat flour, similar to pita bread or corn tortillas

choultry: housing provided by temple authorities near places of pilgrimage in India

D

dagoba: a Buddhist *stupa* or shrine containing a relic

dak bungalow: government rest house

darshan: the vision or experience of a divine form or being

deva: a celestial being

dhal: lentils

Durga Sapthe Sathi: a Sanskrit prayer; 700 *slokas* (verses) of praise to the Goddess Durga

G

ghee: clarified butter

gopuram: tower of a temple

gumfa: a Tibetan Buddhist monastery

Guru Poornima: the holy full moon day in July set aside for paying respect to spiritual teachers, saints and sages

H

halva: an Indian sweet made of semolina or flour

himam: snow

J

jadam: inert (see page 92)

Jagadguru: world preceptor

jaggery: raw sugar

japa: repetition of a *mantra*

K, L

Karma Yoga: performing actions as selfless service without seeking reward

lama: a Tibetan Buddhist monk or priest

M

madam: a monastery

Maha Mrityunjaya Mantra: a prayer for the liberation of all beings

Mahabharata: a Hindu scripture, of which the *Bhagavad Gita* is a part

Makara Sankaranthi: an auspicious day according to the Hindu calendar, marking the end of the six-month period of the year that corresponds to the nighttime of the gods, and proclaiming a new day in heaven

maharishi: (lit.) great sage

mandy: a temporary trading village established in Tibet during the warm months

mantra: a sound formula for meditation

N

nangba: the "divine bird" of Tibetan Buddhism

naya paise: (lit. new cent) a hundredth of an Indian rupee

nirvana: (lit. nakedness) the state of liberation

O

OM: the cosmic sound vibration, which includes all other sounds and vibrations

OM Mani Padme Hum: the *mantra* used by Tibetans meaning "Prayer to *OM*, the Light of Lotus"

OM Tat Sat: "*OM* That is the Truth"

P

pada puja: a worship ceremony performed at the feet of a holy person

parotta: a kind of wheat cake, almost like a *chapathi*

prasadam: consecrated food or other offering; grace

puja: a worship service

Puranas: teachings of the *Vedas* through concrete examples, myths, stories, legends, lives of saints, kings and great men and women, allegories and chronicles of great historical events

puri: a type of Indian flatbread that forms a pocket of air inside when fried

R

rajas: restlessness. One of the three *gunas* controlling nature

rakshasa: a demon

Rama: a name of God

Ramayana: the epic telling the story of Lord Rama as a dutiful son, brother, husband, warrior and king

rishi: a sage

rupee: a unit of Indian currency, equal to approximately US 20 cents in 1958

S

Sama Veda: one of the four main wisdom scriptures of Hinduism

sasthaanga pradakshina: circumambulation done by falling down in full prostration with arms stretched over the head, marking the place where the tips of the fingers are, and standing up, walking to the mark and prostrating again

satsang: spiritual company; a spiritual gathering

Shakti: the Divine Energy, or Divine Mother (see page 92)

shanti: peace

siddha: a highly evolved being, often with supernatural powers

Siva: *God* as auspiciousness (see page 92)

Siva Lingam: the simplest possible form used to represent the Absolute; usually a smooth stone or mound of earth

Sivathandam: the mace of Lord Siva

subji: vegetables

swami: a monk of the Holy Order of *Sannyas*; one who has given up a personal life in order to serve humanity and seek communion with God

T

tapas: (lit. to burn) spiritual austerity; accepting but not causing pain

tharpanam: an offering mainly to the departed souls

trisulam: a trident

Tripitaka: (lit. "Three Baskets") Buddhist scripture comprising 31 books of Buddhist teachings

Y

yagna: sacrifice

Yoga: (lit. union) union of the individual with the Absolute; any spiritual path that makes for such union; unruffled state of mind under all conditions

Sri Swami Satchidananda

Swami Satchidananda (Sri Gurudev) was born on December 22nd in 1914 during the month known as *Margali*, the Dawn of the *Devas*. He was the second son of Sri Kalyanasundaram Gounder and his wife, Srimati Velammai. Their home had always been a meeting place for poets, musicians, philosophers and astrologers. *Sannyasis* (monks) and holy men passing through the area were directed to the home of Sri Kalyanasundaram and Srimati Velammai for food and lodging. Srimati Velammai was inspired by the holy men and decided that her next child should be this type of person. She and her husband traveled sixty miles to Palani, the holy hill, to the Ashram of Sri Sadhu Swamigal, where she was given a *mantra* to invoke the Divine Light as manifested in the Sun. She repeated it constantly, developing a vibration conducive to receiving the type of soul she desired.

From the time he was a little boy, Sri Gurudev (then known as "Ramaswamy") was deeply spiritual. Even as a young child, he spoke truths and displayed insights far beyond his years. His devotion to God was strong, and he looked at people of all castes and faiths with an equal eye, always recognizing the same light within every being. That recognition of the universal light, equally present in all people, remained as he grew to adulthood and became a businessman and a husband.

When he lost his young wife, he turned his attention to spiritual practice and studying with many great spiritual masters, including Sri Ramana Maharshi. Finally, in 1949, Ramaswamy met his Guru–H. H. Sri Swami Sivanandaji of the Divine Life Society, Rishikesh. He received *Sannyas Diksha* (initiation into monkhood) from his spiritual master and was given the name Swami Satchidananda.

So began a new level of dynamic service for Sri Gurudev. Sri Swami Sivanandaji recognized the gift that his newly-initiated *Sannyasin* had for touching the lives of others and did not let this disciple stay in the Rishikesh Ashram for long. Soon, he sent Swami Satchidananda to serve in various parts of India and Sri Lanka. That led to Sri Gurudev's service in many other countries, and eventually–at the insistence of his many American students–to his moving to the United States, as well as to the founding of Satchidananda Ashram–Yogaville, Virginia, and the Integral Yoga Institutes around the world.

Sri Gurudev's message emphasized harmony among people of all races and faiths. His motto was: "Truth is One, Paths are Many." He believed that we are all one in Spirit and that throughout history great spiritual masters, such as Buddha, Moses, and Jesus, have come forward to teach the people of the world how to experience this spiritual oneness. After we have found that Spirit within ourselves, we will always recognize it in others. Then, we truly have power to help heal the world. Sri Gurudev exemplified these teachings. His beautiful message is that we, too, can exemplify them.

Not limited to any one organization, religion or country, Sri Gurudev received invitations for over fifty years from around the world to speak about the way to peace. He served on the advisory boards of numerous Yoga, interfaith and world peace organizations. He received many honors for his public service including, the Albert Schweitzer Humanitarian Award, the Juliet Hollister Interfaith Award and the U Thant Peace Award. In 1999, the 50th anniversary of his ministerial ordination was commemorated during the interfaith service prior to the opening of the 54th General Assembly of the United Nations. Swami Satchidananda dedicated his life to the cause of peace—both individual and universal—and to unity and harmony among all people.

Witnessing the genuine peace and joy experienced by all who participated in these gatherings, Sri Gurudev was inspired to create a permanent place where all people could come to realize their essential oneness. Built in Yogaville, in Central Virginia, the Light Of Truth Universal Shrine (known as LOTUS) is unique in the world because it has altars for all the world faiths. Dedicated to the Light of all faiths and to world peace, the LOTUS is an enduring symbol of unity in diversity. It was completed in 1986 and is open to the public.

Sri Swami Satchidananda entered *Mahasamadhi* on August 19, 2002, in South India. Shortly before leaving the body, he told many people: "*I will always be with you in Spirit. Even if my body is not there, you will never be without me.*" That is what the Yoga tradition teaches us about the ongoing relationship with one's Satguru.